WHO KNOWS

Cavoukian and Tapscott take us on a journey into the dark jungle of information predators...and show us how to come out with our privacy still alive. This book is an invaluable survival tool amid the perils of the wired world.

Bruce Phillips, Privacy Commissioner of Canada

Maintaining privacy in a networked world is a challenge that requires both legal and technical solutions. Cavoukian and Tapscott are both alarming and reassuring in a lucidly presented book.

Esther Dyson, Chair, Electronic Frontier Foundation

A must-read for business leaders who view information as a strategic resource. Cavoukian and Tapscott provide the voice of responsibility and show that a social conscience can actually improve the bottom line.

Mitch Irsfeld, Editor in Chief, Communications Week

Who Knows makes a frightening and convincing case that the average citizen is under attack and better start fighting. Better yet, it offers a compelling list of how-to advice to help Americans regain control over their own private files.

David Klein, Editor, Advertising Age

Cavoukian and Tapscott have laid out a constructive framework to help put the guarantee back in the Fourth Admendment...For every company participating in the digital economy, this book serves as a potent reminder of the vigilance required to protect the fundamental rights of today's information age.

Ward MacKenzie, Vice President,
NYNEX Business Network Solutions

Captivating reading...and it's scary as hell...If you value your privacy, you must protect it. Reading this book is a good place to start. *Brian Greiner,* Computing Canada

WHO KNOWS
Safeguarding Your Privacy in a Networked World

Ann Cavoukian, Ph.D.

Don Tapscott

McGraw-Hill
New York   San Francisco   Washington, D.C.   Auckland   Bogotá
Caracas   Lisbon   London   Madrid   Mexico City   Milan
Montreal   New Delhi   San Juan   Singapore
Sydney   Tokyo   Toronto

Library of Congress Cataloging-in-Publication Data

Cavoukian, Ann.
    Who knows : safeguarding your privacy in a networked world / Ann
Cavoukian, Don Tapscott.
       p.   cm.
    Includes bibliographical references and index.
    ISBN 0-07-063320-7
    1. Privacy, Right of. 2. Information society. 3. Information
technology. I. Tapscott, Don, II. Title.
JC596.C39   1996
323.44'8—dc20   96-24098
                                                             CIP

McGraw-Hill

*A Division of The **McGraw·Hill** Companies*

1 2 3 4 5 6 7 8 9 0 DOC/DOC 9 0 9 8 7 6

ISBN 0-07-063320-7

*The sponsoring editor for this book was Betsy N. Brown, the editing
supervisor was Caroline R. Levine, and the production supervisor was
Donald F. Schmidt. It was set in Fairfield by Ron Painter of McGraw-
Hill's Professional Book Group composition unit.*

Printed and bound by R. R. Donnelley & Sons Company.

This book is printed on acid-free paper.

To my exceptional mother, Lucie Cavoukian,
who has taught me so many of life's lessons

A.C.

To Alex and Nicole Tapscott
that their rights may be safe in the smaller world
they inherit

D.T.

CONTENTS

Part Three. The Future…What's in It for Us?

ACKNOWLEDGMENTS

So many people have assisted in the writing of this book. We are indebted to you all. Among those who gave generously of their time and expertise were three privacy experts who reviewed chapters as they were being written and provided invaluable suggestions: To Colin Bennett, David Flaherty, and James Rule, a heartfelt thanks for all your help and advice. We would also like to thank professors Andrew Clement and Martin Moskovits, and Pierrot Peladeau for reviewing respective chapters and offering strong words of encouragement.

Many thanks to Colin Plumb and Marc Plumb for their help in the area of encryption. We are also grateful to Privacy Commissioners Paul-Andre Comeau, Bruce Phillips, and Tom Wright for their encouragement and support. We also wish to thank the many privacy advocates and colleagues who kindly gave of their time and experience.

To our agent, Bruce Westwood, our original publisher, Doug Pepper, and editor, Shaun Oakey, at Random House of Canada, thanks for your ongoing enthusiasm and for making this book a reality. Thanks also to the McGraw-Hill team: Philip Ruppel, publisher, Betsy Brown, editor, and Caroline Levine, editing supervisor.

On a more personal note, the greatest appreciation goes to our family and friends for their loving support and tireless encouragement. To Linda Bertoldi, Bill Bogart, Ursula Hunter, Krishna Khalsa, Svetlana Kurnew, Michael Lunney, Caren and Gary McCracken, Antoinette Schatz, Gilbert Sharpe, Carol and John Shelly, and Jody Stevens: we are truly grateful for your thoughtfulness and patience. A very special thanks to Raffi Cavoukian for being an unwavering source of hope and inspiration; to Kim MacNeil for her unfailing support and friendship; and to Maureen Webster who tirelessly read each chapter as it was being written (and always said it was great; what a friend!). And to the Cavoukian and Tapscott clans, much love and thanks for putting up with so much yet never wavering in your faith and support.

Ann Cavoukian
Don Tapscott

PRIVACY AND TECHNOLOGY: NOTHING STAYS THE SAME

Introduction

The New Technologies, the New Economy, the New World

Individually, most new technologies are introduced for perfectly benign motives. Their cumulative effect, however, is to cast a shadow over personal privacy. Is it really acceptable for most of your actions, even the most mundane, to be recorded and then sold to the highest bidder?...If your answer is a shrug of indifference, turn the page. You have nothing to fear. You are also likely to be in a minority. Most people take their privacy for granted but are outraged when it is breached.

Economist, 1993

Why should you worry about losing your privacy? Because privacy as we now know it may not exist in the year 2000. Rapid developments in technology are bringing dramatic changes, changes that will affect the privacy you may now take for granted. Consider the following scenario.

You check into a hospital to get the much-needed treatment you need for a serious drinking problem. You've finally come to accept the fact that you need to get professional help to detox. But you've decided not to tell your family about it. After all, you've managed to keep it from them so far, so why distress them now? You live alone, you work from home, so nobody needs to know. And of course, you take it for granted that your hospital records will remain completely confidential. Think again.

3

What you don't know is that it is quite common for clerks and other hospital personnel to browse through patient records. Since records are mostly computerized now, it's easy to do and it helps pass the monotony of the midnight shift. One clerk who was in the habit of browsing happened to stumble across your file. It turns out that she lives down the street from your parents, so your name caught her attention. Assuming that they knew, she sent them a sympathy card saying she would do whatever she could to make your stay as comfortable as possible, especially since going through DTs can be a horrendous ordeal. End of confidentiality...end of deciding who knows...end of control.

If you happen to be a celebrity, however, you might have a greater chance of preserving your privacy. Ralph Nader suspected as much—that celebrities are given special protection by those keeping volumes of information about people, and he was right. At least two American hospitals do just that. The University of Maryland Hospital in Baltimore took great care in designing its patient database to prevent employees without "a need to know" from browsing through patient records. An additional access code is required for staff to view the files of VIPs or hospital employees. "To gain access, a staff member must answer a special question not required for access to records about common patients: 'Are you involved in the care of this patient?'"[1] Requiring employees to identify themselves and coupling this with an audit trail that can trace who has accessed what records (with strong penalties for unauthorized access) presents a strong deterrent against idle browsing through patient records.

At the Beth Israel Hospital affiliated with Harvard Medical School, an electronic tag is attached to the names of patients to identify those whose records have a "higher-than-normal risk of being looked at."[2] Famous patients are also permitted to use a pseudonym or false name. While this may be highly desirable if you're a VIP, it still leaves at risk the records of common patients (the great majority of us). Surely the protection of your medical records should not hinge on the ability to demonstrate special status.

Or consider the next scenario. The holiday season has just ended, and once again you notice that you ate too much. So you sign yourself into a 2-week weight-loss clinic. To your delight, you manage to lose 7 pounds during that time. The next week a package arrives in the mail. You open it and find 6 delectable chocolates—a sample offering of Company X's truffles—and a special-offer-only-for-you coupon. Could this just be an uncanny coincidence? No, it is not. Unknown to you, and without your consent, the weight-loss clinic routinely sells its customer list to the chocolate company. After all, it probably increases both their businesses. But should marketers be allowed to take advantage of vulnerable individuals? No. Is there anything you can do about it? Yes.

Profound changes are taking place around us every day, even though we may be oblivious to them. This should come as no surprise, since many of the changes are very subtle, occurring as isolated instances, here and there, each case appearing to be the exception. It is their cumulative effect that concerns us. Other changes, however, are too significant to overlook.

It is clear that a new economy is emerging. This won't be the first time we have witnessed how a major change in our economic structure brings about significant social changes. When we shifted from an agrarian society to an industry-based economy, farmwork dropped from 80 percent to 3 percent of all jobs. The current transformation from an industrial economy to a "knowledge" economy may be equally dramatic. The new knowledge-based economy will be "digital" because it is based on networked communications—companies will be doing business online. The infrastructure for this new form of economic activity is the computer network, the bedrock of future economic development. There is a growing consensus in business, government, and many public interest groups that the so-called information highway will be the key to future economic and social success, both for businesses and for individuals. Just think of how current technology is profoundly changing the way we work, learn, do business, bank, shop, and entertain ourselves. In the United States, business publications are striving to make their corporate readers aware of the massive shift that is under way. Every major business publication has devoted entire issues to telling employers why they should open their eyes to the new networked, chip-driven economy. As *Fortune* magazine said of the new economy, "Embrace it, for it will transform our lives and the way we work, more profoundly than we can imagine—and nothing is going to stop it."

Economic success will no longer be based on manufacturing, natural resources, and hard work. The new networked economy will be driven by the transfer of information and "know-how," and the ability to apply this to every aspect of our lives. In a knowledge-based economy, having the proper information tools will become essential. But how will they be distributed?

Staggering social issues are raised by the new technologies. How will we achieve such things as universality of access, a long-held principle when it comes to telephones? Will we have a society of information "haves" and have-nots? Of the information-rich and information-poor? And what about privacy? How will we preserve our privacy in a networked world?

Protection of privacy is not just a moral or social issue; it is also an emerging business imperative. It makes sense for businesses to tackle this issue proactively, to gain a competitive advantage through enlightened approaches to the privacy of their customers, employees, and markets. Various interest groups also have a stake in how these issues are resolved—community groups, civil rights organizations, political parties, unions. And government has a significant role to play.

If the emergence of our networked world was left to the exclusive control of the private sector, there would be little assurance of preserving the privacy we now take for granted. As Don Tapscott wrote in *On Ramp: Your Guide to the Information Highway*, "An information infrastructure shaped solely by the marketplace could have ugly consequences. Computers could record whom we telephone, what movies we watch, databases we use, goods we buy, and more. In an unfettered, wired world, the marriage of telecommunications to databases could destroy our privacy."[3]

Similar views were expressed by Canada's privacy commissioner, Bruce Phillips, in his *1994 Annual Report*. (The United States doesn't have a privacy commissioner; it should.)

> The term [information highway] undoubtedly implies linking up vast sources of information by computers and telecommunications, and making that information available to vastly increased numbers of people....Unless some sensible rules of traffic management are a part of these systems, the first roadkill will be our personal privacy and dignity....These are not alarmist observations. On the contrary, it is difficult to exaggerate the potential consequences of carelessness or indifference to privacy in this looming new environment.

If the new economy will be going online, so will the public through its increasing use of credit and debit cards, computers, and telecommunications networks. Every purchase you make, every telephone call you place, every electronic-mail message you send, and every voice-mail message you receive will leave behind a detailed digital trail that will become trapped in a variety of computer databases, easily accessible by others through the growing web of electronic networks.

Today, perhaps more than ever, information is power. In a free and democratic society, however, power must ultimately rest with the people. In the words of Bruce Phillips, "Privacy is essential to maintaining a free society. It is fundamental to the democratic notion of self-determination or autonomy—of retaining control over our lives. It is at the heart of the concept that the individual is not the instrument of the state or, it needs underlining, the marketplace, but the reverse."

The concept of privacy is tied to the very fabric of democracy; the erosion of one may lead to the erosion of the other. If you want to keep your power on the information highway and protect your privacy, you need to be aware of how your privacy can be taken away from you, quietly, invisibly, easily. It is already being chipped away, little by little, every day. As early as 1980, David Burnham, in his classic work *The Rise of the Computer State*, sounded the alarm:

> Computers and telecommunications enormously enhance the ability of organizations to collect, store, collate, and dis-

tribute all kinds of information about virtually all of the 232 million people in the United States. Computers have allowed far more organizations to have far more access to far more people at far less cost than ever was possible in the age of the manual file and the wizened file clerk.[4]

Burnham wrote this in prenetwork times, before the days of easy access to high-speed networked communications and a PC on every desk and in every home; before the days of interactive TV and multimedia. One can imagine the possibilities now, and hope that privacy doesn't come as an afterthought.

In the chapters that follow, we propose a variety of ways for you to gain control over your privacy. Government regulation is only one of several solutions we will look at. We examine various areas that pose threats to our privacy, and the parties who should be involved in protecting it—government, industry, business, designers of technology, and most important you, the individual.

In Chapters 2 and 3, we examine the meaning of privacy and why it means different things to different people. We view privacy as a fundamental human right, much needed in a free and democratic society. So we begin by exploring the relationship of privacy to the state (the role played by government), and look at how government has tended to approach the protection of privacy, especially when it is balanced against other values. We also describe a set of practices that, when applied to personal information, result in its fair and responsible treatment.

In Chapter 4, we provide a brief overview of privacy laws in the United States, Canada, and Europe. We discuss how the new European Union (EU) may affect business conducted with non-EU countries when exchanges of personal information are involved.

Chapter 5 reviews how the growth of computers has led to the rise of surveillance, which leads directly into Chapter 6 on the Internet and the information highway. We try to give you a glimpse of the future, and what you might expect to find when living in a networked world.

Chapter 7 looks at consumer privacy—your privacy when dealing with the marketplace. We report that numerous surveys and polls show that people have become increasingly concerned about their privacy. We discuss the value of your information—that it's worth a great deal more than you may think and that you should consider getting paid for its use. We also review database marketing and direct marketing and explore how these can jeopardize your privacy. We provide suggestions for what you, as consumers, can do to protect your privacy in your day-to-day transactions.

Chapter 8 explores the area of medical privacy, or lack thereof, and the confidentiality of your medical records. (Some refer to this as the "myth of confidentiality.") Chapter 9 looks at privacy in the workplace. Should there be any? Is your boss free to pry into your personal life? Can your boss monitor every move you make, on and off the job?

In Chapter 10, we contrast the technologies of privacy with the technologies of surveillance. We review a number of technological solutions to privacy that counterbalance the intrusive direction that technology has taken us thus far. We show that technology can help to protect privacy just as it can lead to its demise. The choice is ultimately yours to make.

In Chapter 11, we tell business why it should listen to people's fears of losing their privacy—why it should treat them seriously. We tell businesspeople why they would be wise to build privacy protection into their day-to-day operations—not just because it's the right thing to do, but because it will give them a definite edge over their competitors.

The final chapter is a call to action. Chapter 12 summarizes the solutions proposed for protecting your privacy—ranging from government regulation, industry-developed privacy codes, personal and corporate responsibility, and technological solutions that build in privacy protection from the first step, to the need for public education and awareness. The book ends, as it began, by emphasizing that privacy revolves around choice—your ability to choose. The importance of preserving choice in a free and democratic society cannot be overstated: the choice of keeping your private life private, the choice of keeping your personal information confidential. As Canada's privacy commissioner warns, "It's our choice, and we are fast running out of time."

ENDNOTES

1. Robert Ellis Smith, "Some Are More Equal Than Others," *Privacy Journal*, Vol. 22, No. 1 (November 1995), p. 4.

2. Ibid.

3. Don Tapscott, "How to Avoid Information Apartheid," in *On Ramp: Your Guide to the Information Highway* (Toronto: Globe and Mail, 1994), p. 10.

4. David Burnham, *The Rise of the Computer State: The Threat to Our Freedoms, Our Ethics and Our Democratic Process* (New York: Random House, 1980), p. 11.

First Things First:
A Privacy Primer

*Every time you make a telephone call, purchase goods using a
credit card, subscribe to a magazine, or pay your taxes, that information goes into a database somewhere. Furthermore, all these
records can be linked so that they constitute in effect a single
dossier on your life—not only your medical and financial history
but also what you buy, where you travel, and whom you communicate with. It is almost impossible to learn the full extent of the
files that various organizations keep on you, much less to assure
their accuracy or to control who may gain access to them.*

DAVID CHAUM
Achieving Electronic Privacy, 1992

What is privacy? It is something that we enjoy every day; that
we take for granted; that we would miss if we didn't have. Most
people have a sense of what privacy is but have a hard time
putting it into words. Privacy is easy to recognize, but difficult
to describe. Ask people to define it and you will get a number
of different responses. But perhaps this should come as no surprise, since there are so many different definitions of privacy.

Definitions of privacy have been as simple as the well-
known words of Louis Brandeis of the United States Supreme
Court in 1890: "the right to be let alone." But privacy has also
been defined comprehensively:

Privacy is a concept related to solitude, secrecy, and autonomy, but it is not synonymous with these terms; for beyond
the purely descriptive aspects of privacy as isolation from
the company, the curiosity, and the influence of others, privacy implies a normative element: the right to exclusive con-

trol of access to private realms...the right to privacy asserts the sacredness of the person;...any invasion of privacy constitutes an offense against the rights of the personality—against individuality, dignity, and freedom.[1]

Other definitions of privacy have included:

- "The extent to which we are known to others, the extent to which others have physical access to us, and the extent to which we are the subject of others' attention."[2]

- "A degree of inaccessibility of persons, of their mental states, and of information about them to the senses and surveillance devices of others."[3]

- "The claim of individuals, groups, or institutions to determine for themselves when, how, and to what extent information about them is communicated to others."[4]

One thing is for certain: privacy is a very subjective concept. For some, it revolves around human dignity and respect, freedom from interference or intrusion, and preservation of personal autonomy. An important component of protecting privacy is maintaining control over the information that is circulating about you—informational privacy.

For others, privacy means placing restrictions on outside access to their private world, keeping their physical space exclusively to themselves—territorial privacy (as in building a fence around your house).

Another type of privacy—privacy of the person—is privacy associated with intrusions into one's body, ranging from requests to surrender bodily specimens and fluids to bodily examinations and physical searches. Then there are the various categories of privacy associated with specific sectors: communications privacy, workplace privacy, medical privacy, genetic privacy, and physical privacy, to name a few.

Perhaps Louis Brandeis' definition of privacy is the best, in that it captures the essence of privacy in its simplest form: "the right to be let alone." It reflects the broad scope that the concept of privacy has to some people. For those in the public eye, such as the late Jacqueline Kennedy Onassis or the royal family, the longing for privacy may simply reflect their wish to be left alone. Jackie Kennedy knew how much privacy meant to her and fought hard to preserve it. She valued her privacy enormously. She knew how important it was, perhaps because she was so often without it in the public eye—a place where privacy does not come naturally. So Jackie Kennedy could not take her privacy for granted.

But most of us are not in the public eye, so we may not be able to grasp the importance of privacy until we experience how things are, or might be, in a world without it. David Flaherty, an internationally renowned expert on privacy and data protection, has said: "Privacy is like freedom: we do not recognize its importance until it is taken away."

Clearly, the time to ensure the protection of your privacy (much like your freedom) is while you still have it—while you can still enjoy it, every day. Because once your privacy is taken away from you, it is much harder to get it back.

What Does Privacy Mean to You?

Take a moment to think about your own life. Does it matter that you are able to maintain a private life, separate and apart from your public or work life? Are there some things that you want to share only with those closest to you, or with no one at all? Think of things such as transcripts containing poor grades from school, a suicide attempt, thoughts of leaving your spouse, a severe depression, a personal bankruptcy, having an affair, or responding to a personals ad.

Do you want your friends and neighbors to know how much money you make, or that you never paid off your student loan? What about past brushes with the law? What about the details of your medical history: that you had an abortion 10 years ago; that you're seeing a psychotherapist; that you've had a sexually transmitted disease; that you're receiving treatment for impotence; that you're on the pill and you work for a Catholic schoolboard; that you're taking Prozac or AZT; that you're seeing a doctor for a prostate condition; that you've had breast cancer and wear a prosthesis; that you're seeing a doctor for penile treatment; that you're seeking treatment for incontinence; that you've had an HIV test?

Or what about your children—their learning disabilities, speech impediments, poor IQ test scores, history of substance abuse, or reports of antisocial behavior at school?

What about any personal preferences you may have that, while quite legal, would be frowned upon if known by others (such as your boss)? Have you ever had an HIV test? (If you're single and dating, we certainly hope so; but should it be anyone's business but your own?)

As Evan Hendricks, editor of *Privacy Times*, says, "You go through life dropping little bits of data about yourself everywhere. Following right after you are big vacuum cleaners sucking them up." The vacuum cleaners may take many forms, but you should have some control over what they pick up.

Democracy, Freedom, Privacy

In response to whether you should mind being asked personal questions, people often say: "Well, if you don't have anything to hide...." But it's not a matter of having something to hide. It's about exercising our right to decide for ourselves whom we choose to share the personal details of our lives with. In a democracy, the starting point is not one where everybody is supposed to know everything about everybody else. Nor is the state supposed to know everything about us. That's how it works in a fascist or totalitarian state, but not in a democracy. In a democracy, we have voted in favor of human rights and civil liberties, in favor of freedom, in favor of privacy.

In a democracy, citizens have many freedoms. We can hold a wide range of political views, religious beliefs, views on the economy, opinions on how our schools should be run, views on the environment and on our health care system, you name it. Freedom of thought is intrinsic to a democracy.

Privacy protects that freedom of thought. With privacy intact, you can pick when, where, and with whom you choose to share your views. That's what freedom is all about, free will and self-determination. *You* get to decide—not the state, not the police, not your boss, not your mother, not your partner, not your friends, not your neighbors.

Perhaps the only way to truly appreciate privacy is to imagine what life would be like without it. In *Big Brother*, Simon Davies writes: "People who have no rights of privacy are vulnerable to limitless intrusions by governments, corporations, or anyone else who chooses to interfere in your personal affairs. Imagine a world where government had an unfettered right to demand information from you, or to remove money from your bank account, or even to enter your house. The tragic history of many of the world's countries shows us that a nation denied the right of privacy is invariably denied all other freedoms and rights."[5]

A Matter of Balance

The state—through various arms of government—is one of the two main sources of intrusion into our private lives. (The other is the private sector, through commercial transactions. This will be discussed in Chapter 7.)

A December 11, 1993 editorial in Canada's *Globe and Mail* captured the essence of the relationship: "The state is the creation of a self-governing people. We do not have such rights as the state allots us; rather, it has such powers, and only such powers, as we consent to give it. All rights not expressly limited are reserved to the people; all powers not expressly granted are denied. It is never incumbent on the people to show why they should have rights; the burden of proof is always on those who would restrict them."

In his excellent work on privacy protection in the United States and Europe, *Regulating Privacy*, Colin Bennett reminds us that the state is composed of its citizens and has no superior role: "Government is constituted by citizens and should remain accountable to them, from the conduct of the most significant public policy, down to the management of the most insignificant piece of personal information."[6]

The proper relationship between individuals and society regarding the balancing of rights, responsibilities and the powers of the state can be debated at some length. However, when it comes to privacy, the questions can be as simple as: How much of your personal information should the government have? How much is it lawfully permitted to have? The answers usually depend on how much information it really needs, and what it needs to use that information for.

There are no easy answers. What complicates matters is that a number of other values compete with privacy. An individual's right to privacy may conflict with the collective rights of the public. For example, as a society we value the need for administrative efficiency in our government. With that, however, comes greater scrutiny, to make sure that resources are being properly spent and that only those who are truly eligible for government programs and services actually receive them.

Obviously, there are times when some of your personal information is legitimately needed to obtain a desired service (like getting health services or a driver's license) or to ensure compliance with something that is in the public interest (like paying your share of taxes). But just where to draw the line is not an easy matter. And depending on your background, your cultural, personal, and political views, each of you may draw the line at a different place.

We do not suggest that privacy is an absolute right that reigns supreme over all other rights. It does not. However, the case for privacy will depend on a number of factors that can influence the balance—the level of harm to the individual involved versus the needs of the public. Consider a convicted child abuser about to be released from prison. If protecting his identity and criminal record is viewed as being harmful to the children in the community he will be living in, then the need to protect his privacy (identity) is not as great as the need to protect society from the potential harm it perceives.

On the other hand, protecting the identity of a person who is HIV-positive ranks high. Since the virus cannot be transmitted by casual contact (e.g., talking to someone, working next to someone), the harm to the public in not knowing this information is virtually nonexistent. The opposite is true for the HIV-positive person: the harm in having this information disclosed is extremely high, since it can be used to discriminate against him or her. It can lead to loss of employment, loss of benefits, and loss of accommodation, to name but a few of the consequences. Therefore, where the harm to the individual in disclosure is high and the harm to the public is low, protection of privacy is paramount.

What About the Police?

> Law enforcement...would be wonderfully efficient if there were no rights to privacy—if all of the information about every citizen which is possessed by the state were centrally stored and easily accessible, if the agents of the state could at will search any person or home and seize any evidence which might relate to a crime, and bug any telephone or office. This is a description of a totalitarian state. Such sweeping powers of search and surveillance are not tolerated in a democratic society.[7]

The right to privacy may often conflict with efficient law enforcement. If the police could know more about the activities of the "undesirable elements" of our society, then they would be in a better position to eliminate crime. But determining who falls into the "undesirable" category is not an exact science. Police intelligence units try to figure out who the "bad guys" are and then keep track of them, gathering information for the purpose of maintaining "security." (Such intelligence-gathering activities are unrelated to the investigation of specific incidents of wrongdoing.) The reach is broad, as a comment by one police chief reflects: "From time to time, intelligence checks out everything about anybody, including myself." This comment was in response to the allegation that the police had compiled a secret file on the civilian head of the police commission—a woman with whom the chief often clashed.

An example of police intelligence gone awry illustrates the potential for harm. In the late 1960s and the 1970s, the Royal Canadian Mounted Police (RCMP) compiled racist "spy" reports on two supposed black activists. Detailed files containing derogatory racial comments about the two black people were the result of an extensive undercover operation arising from a concern that the U.S. Black Panthers were "inciting violence" in eastern Canada.

The two subjects recalled numerous incidents of their mail being tampered with and their telephones cut off. They believed that the RCMP had been involved. They also felt that the surveillance operations had impeded their career prospects and their attempts to get financial credit.

In 1994 the head of the RCMP finally apologized for the derogatory remarks and publicly stated, "Some files from that period contained racial stereotypes and portrayed members of the black community in a derogatory manner. I do not condone such comments in any way and must state clearly that the RCMP deeply regrets and apologizes for the negative reflection that this has had on the black community."[8]

The compilation of intelligence reports and political dossiers by law enforcement agencies, often in the absence of any reasonable suspicion of criminal activity, may not be new, but should continue to alarm us. One need only think back to the extensive, damaging files kept by the late J. Edgar Hoover when he was director of the Federal Bureau of Investigation (FBI). Or need we remind you of the McCarthy era and the witchhunt that took place in the 1950s in the search for communist sympathizers?

A somewhat amusing, if not astounding, quote about the FBI was discovered by David Seipp in his chronicling of the right to privacy in American history. In 1931, a spokesman for the FBI was asked whether the agency would ever think of using wiretapping. He dismissed such an outlandish proposition by answering: "No, sir. We have a very definite rule in the bureau that any employee engaging in wiretapping will be dismissed from the service of the bureau....While it may not be illegal, I think it is unethical, and it is not permitted under the regulations by the Attorney General."[9] That spokesman was J. Edgar Hoover.

Not only did Hoover resort to wiretapping people's telephone conversations but he went on to use a wide range of surveillance techniques to compile dossiers on leading (and not-so-leading) figures in the United States. But sometimes less than successfully, as the following example illustrates.

The FBI had consistently denied keeping files on members of Congress except when a criminal investigation was under way. On one occasion, the bureau was giving members of the House Judiciary Committee a tour of its offices. One congressman noticed the drawer of a filing cabinet marked with the first three letters of his last name. He opened it and found information on him dating back to 1958.

There might well be times when intelligence agencies have good reason to compile dossiers on members of the public. There are other times, however, when we are hard-pressed to imagine why public funds would be expended on these activities. In 1983, a sixth-grade student in New Jersey wrote 169 letters to various countries, to obtain information for a school project; the return address he used was his father's business address. The FBI, unaware of the reason for so much mail being received from all over the world (although the bureau could have asked), started keeping a file on the activity. Even after the FBI realized that a student was innocently responsible, it continued amassing this file for another 2 years. The family believed that its mail was being intercepted and its telephone calls tapped. Equally remarkable, the student was not permitted access to his own file—for reasons of national security.

Clearly, the subjects of intelligence surveillance can easily be ordinary, law-abiding people like you or your children. If you voice an alternative opinion, join a particular type of group, or even write letters to foreign countries, you may become a target. And a record of any charges laid may be retained in a centralized computer database like NCIC (National Criminal Information Center) or CPIC (Canadian Police Information Center), which can be accessed by any police agency, anywhere in the country. Databases, however, are fraught with errors, and large databases such as the NCIC or CPIC, which contain millions and millions of computer records, are especially prone to inaccuracy. Not a very comforting thought if erroneous information about you finds its way into these databases, which are not presently subject to any form of systematic oversight.

Secret files relate very much to the central concern of this book, informational privacy. One of the best definitions of informational privacy comes from the "father of privacy," Professor Alan Westin, in his seminal work, *Privacy and Freedom*: "the claim of individuals, groups, or institutions to determine for themselves when, how, and to what extent information about them is communicated to others."[10] We would take it one step further by including "if"—*if* personal information should be collected or gathered in the first place.

The next time someone says to you, "What do you have to hide?" simply reply, "Why do you want to know?" Take the offensive by asking, "Why do you need my personal information? What gives you the right to ask for my information?" It is up to the requester of the information to justify the request. Refuse to be put on the defensive—you shouldn't have to defend your privacy. Remember, when people want something that belongs to you, they would normally buy it or borrow it. At the very least, they would ask you for it and tell you why they wanted it. The same must apply to your personal information.

If from this day forward you ask one simple question each time someone asks you for your information, you will make an enormous difference. This is no exaggeration. Simply ask, "Why do you want this information? What do you intend to use it for?" and people's attitudes will start to change. If enough of us do this, we will witness a transformation. With time, people will come to tell you, without being asked, why they need your personal information. Better still, they will first have to think about it. We suspect that in many cases they won't really know why the information is needed. Reject the pat response "It's company policy; we've always asked for it; we need to keep it on file." Ask why their policy requires it and why it needs to be kept on file. Often there is no good reason, and the request for your personal information will be withdrawn. Mission accomplished.

Concluding Thought

Each chapter will end with a single thought that we would like to stay with you. If you remember nothing else, remember the last thought.

It's not a matter of having something to hide. Turn the question around: Why do they need your personal information? How do they intend to use it? Make sure you get good answers to these questions. Speak up and challenge the routine expectation that you must relinquish your information to anyone who asks for it. You do not.

Endnotes

1. Arnold Simmel, quoted in David H. Flaherty, *Protecting Privacy in Surveillance Societies* (Chapel Hill: University of North Carolina Press, 1989), p. 9.

2. Ruth Gavison, quoted in *Philosophical Dimensions of Privacy: An Anthology,* ed. Ferdinand D. Schoeman (Cambridge, Eng.: Cambridge University Press, 1984), p. 379.

3. Anita Allen, quoted in Sheri Alpert, "Smart Cards, Smarter Policy: Medical Records, Privacy, and Health Care Reform," *Hastings Center Report,* Vol. 23, No. 6 (1993), p. 19.

4. Alan F. Westin, *Privacy and Freedom* (New York: Atheneum, 1967), p. x.

5. Simon Davies, *Big Brother: Australia's Growing Web of Surveillance* (Sydney: Simon and Schuster, 1992), pp. 5–6.

6. Colin J. Bennett, *Regulating Privacy: Data Protection and Public Policy in Europe and the United States* (Cornell University Press, 1992), p. 31.

7. Erin Shaw, John Westwood, and Russell Wodell, *The Privacy Handbook* (Vancouver: 1994), p. 23.

8. Alan Young, quoted by Gail Swainson, "Report Slams Metro Police for Dossiers on Black Activists," *Toronto Star,* June 24, 1994.

9. David J. Seipp, *The Right to Privacy in American History* (Cambridge, Mass.: Harvard University Press, 1978), p. 108.

10. Westin, *Privacy and Freedom,* p. x.

Informational Privacy and Fair Information Practices

Information privacy means different things to different people. In venturing to define it, I am tempted to borrow the observation made by Supreme Court Justice Potter Stewart, who when confronted with a case involving obscenity, said he could not define obscenity, "but I know it when I see it." I think we all know the abuse of information privacy when we see it.   DAVID F. LINOWES
Privacy in America, 1989

Most of this book explores the protection of your privacy as it relates to information about you that others may want (but you may not want to give)—that is, informational privacy. Personal information is any information about you that is identifiable as yours, meaning that it has your name or an identifying number (like your social security number) attached to it. So your personal information is your name plus any of the following: your address, telephone number, age, sex, medical records, psychiatric history, blood type, genetic history, prescription profile, fingerprints, criminal record, credit rating, race, religion, ethnic origin, sexual orientation, marital status, education, place of work, employment history, personal interests, favorite movies, lifestyle preferences, and much more. What you read and say and buy and watch can be telling—it may reveal a great deal. Keeping all this information from prying eyes appears to be getting harder and harder.

A fundamental premise underlying democratic societies such as ours is an individual's right to autonomy—the right to be free and self-directing. The right to be autonomous means that you get to decide what choices you want to make. You get to control your private life, and the decisions you make are your own. Yet with the growth of large organizations and staggering advances in technology, it is harder to maintain that control, to remain truly autonomous and self-directing.

The ability to determine the fate of one's personal information is so important in Germany that in 1983 the Constitutional Court ruled that all citizens had the right to what is called "informational self-determination." Individuals, not the government, determine the fate of their personal information. The eminent privacy scholar and former data protection commissioner of the German state of Hesse, Spiros Simitis, stated: "Since this ruling...it has been an established fact in this country that the Constitution gives the individual the right to decide when and under what circumstances his personal data may be processed."[1]

In his insightful book *Protecting Privacy in Surveillance Societies,* David Flaherty, outlines a number of privacy interests that people might hold about themselves. These include:

- The right to individual autonomy
- The right to a private life
- The right to control information about oneself
- The right to limit accessibility
- The right to exclusive control of access to private realms
- The right to expect confidentiality
- The right to enjoy solitude
- The right to enjoy intimacy
- The right to enjoy reserve
- The right to secrecy

What all these aspects of privacy have in common is not only freedom from prying eyes but, more important, the ability to control—to make choices about—who is allowed to look into your private life or have access to your personal information.

(Remember your personal information belongs to you, no one else. Governments, banks, and other organizations that need your information often forget that they act only as custodians of the information which you entrust to them, and which they are responsible for safekeeping. They do not own it.)

But why should you care if someone can get hold of this information about you?

Internationally Recognized Privacy Principles

In 1980, the Organization for Economic Cooperation and Development (OECD) developed a set of practices to ensure the fair treatment and handling of personal information collected by organizations. These principles are commonly referred to as the Code of Fair Information Practices (FIPs), and they are the basis of virtually all privacy legislation worldwide.[2]

The essence of Fair Information Practices is quite simple:

- Only the information that is really needed should be collected.
- Where possible, it should be collected directly from the individual to whom it pertains (the data subject).
- The data subject should be told why the information is needed.
- The information should be used only for the intended purpose.
- The information should not be used for other (secondary) purposes without the data subject's consent.
- Data subjects should be given the opportunity to see their personal information and correct it if it's wrong.

FIPs are directed at anyone wishing to obtain your personal information—that is, data users. Data users tend to be large organizations such as government agencies or private sector enterprises such as banks and insurance companies, but the term applies to any individual, group, or organization, large or small, that wishes to obtain your information.

FIPs impose certain responsibilities on data users. In exchange for your information, users must follow a series of rules when using it. Restrictions are placed, for instance, on how data users are permitted to obtain the information. Either they must have the legal authority to do so (since the law requires you to pay taxes, the government has the legal authority to ask you how much money you make) or they must "need" the information in order to perform their duties (they can't send you your refund check if they don't have your address).

Collection and Use Limitation

Perhaps the most important FIPs have to do with limitations on how much of your personal information may be collected (with your consent, where possible) and how it may be used. The use limitation is the bedrock of privacy-protective practices in that it restricts the use of the information collected to that which was specified to you at the time of the collection. This is the "primary" purpose of the collection—the main reason for seeking it—as distinct from any subsequent "secondary" uses of the information (which you as the data subject would not know of, since such uses were not identified at the time of the collection). The importance of this restriction cannot be overemphasized. It requires that the data user use the information for essentially one purpose only, and prohibits the user from disclosing (as in selling or renting) personal information to third parties for additional, secondary purposes.

Openness and Transparency

Another FIP talks about the need for openness in the data users' information practices. It requires that you, as the data subject, know how your information is to be used. The conditions under which personal information are held should be "transparent." Transparency here means that you should be able to see clearly the uses your information is being put to, as well as the practices being applied to it.

Two other FIPs state that your information should be protected by reasonable security safeguards and that only accurate and up-to-date information should be used. It is possible to check this only if an organization is open about its policies—if its practices are transparent. That is one reason openness and transparency are so important. Transparency also serves as a strong deterrent to secrecy.

Data Quality and Security

The requirement that personal data be accurate, relevant to the purposes for which it is used, and up-to-date becomes even more important in this day of advanced computers and networked communications. Once your information has been used inappropriately or stored inaccurately, these errors will be spread whenever the information is electronically transmitted to others and retained in countless databases. Once that happens, you have lost all control over your personal information. Strong security safeguards are needed to contain the damage that could result from unauthorized access to your information, its unauthorized destruction or modification, or its disclosure to third parties for secondary purposes. With the growth of networked communications, technical safeguards to protecting your privacy will assume a far greater role.

Individual Participation and Accountability

The right of access to your own information is a fundamental premise underlying privacy protection, for the ability to maintain control over your personal information would not be possible if you couldn't know what information about you was being held in various databases by various organizations. You would not be able to verify its uses, nor would you be able to check its accuracy. For these reasons, data subjects must be permitted access to their information, within a reasonable time and in an intelligible form (i.e., in legible words rather than binary computer code), and permitted to correct erroneous data. If a request for access is denied, the data subject must be given a reason for the denial and the opportunity to appeal the decision to a data controller, who is ultimately accountable.

The final principle in FIPs in fact talks about accountability. There should be someone within the organization responsible for making sure that Fair Information Practices are followed (the data controller). This person is held accountable for ensuring that the company's FIPs are followed. The best policies in the world are of little value if they are ignored. They must be taken seriously and implemented properly. Assigning a high-ranking individual to be acountable for Fair Information Practices within an organization will make people take notice. It will also lead to the successful implementation of those practices.

The complete set of eight principles contained in the OECD's Code of Fair Information Practices may be found below.

OECD Guidelines for the Protection of Privacy and Transborder Flows of Personal Data

COLLECTION LIMITATION.   Collection should be limited to personal data; data should be obtained by lawful and fair means and, where appropriate, with the knowledge or consent of the data subject.

DATA QUALITY.   Personal data should be relevant to the purposes for which it is to be used and, to the extent necessary for those purposes, should be accurate, complete, and up-to-date.

PURPOSE SPECIFICATION.   The purposes for which personal data are collected should be specified not later than at the time of data collection, and the subsequent use limited to the fulfillment of those purposes or such others as are not incompatible with those purposes and as are specified on each occasion of change of purpose.

USE LIMITATION.   Personal data should not be disclosed, made available, or otherwise used for purposes other than those specified (purpose specification) except (a) with the consent of the data subject or (b) by the authority of law.

SECURITY SAFEGUARDS.   Personal data should be protected by reasonable security safeguards against such risks as loss of unauthorized access, destruction, use, modification, or disclosure of data.

OPENNESS.   There should be a general policy of openness about developments, practices, and policies with respect to personal data. Means should be readily available for establishing the existence and nature of personal data, and the main purpose of their use, as well as the identity and usual residence of the data controller.

INDIVIDUAL PARTICIPATION.   An individual should have the right:

(a) to obtain from a data controller, or otherwise, confirmation of whether or not the data controller has data relating to him;
(b) to have communicated to him, data relating to him:
    (i)   within a reasonable time;
    (ii)   at a charge, if any, that is not excessive;
    (iii) in a reasonable manner; and
    (iv)   in a form that is readily intelligible to him;
(c) to be given reasons if a request made under subparagraphs (a) and (b) is denied, and to be able to challenge denial; and
(d) to challenge data relating to him and, if the challenge is successful, to have data erased, rectified, completed, or amended.

ACCOUNTABILITY.   A data controller should be accountable for complying with measures which give effect to the principles stated above.

At first glance, these principles may seem like common sense. However, they are rarely practiced without some type of enforcement mechanism. Armed with the simple knowledge of these FIPs, you will know what questions to ask those seeking your personal information. Perhaps you will find yourself making use of them daily. We'll tell you exactly what to ask and how to frame your questions in Chapter 7, on consumer privacy.

Privacy versus Confidentiality: What's the Difference?

People often confuse privacy with confidentiality and use the terms interchangeably. But they are not one and the same. Privacy is a much broader concept that extends well beyond the limited protection offered by confidentiality.

Privacy involves the right to exercise control over your personal information. Perhaps the most important aspect of this control is its collection—deciding whom you're going to give your information to. Privacy protection imposes restrictions on the collection, storage, use, and dissemination of personal information. Confidentiality, on the other hand, provides only one means of protecting that information, in the form of keeping it secure from prying eyes. So when you think of privacy, think of a broad range of protections. When you think of confidentiality, think of safekeeping and security.

The difference between the broader privacy protection and confidentiality is important, because once your personal information is collected, it may be too late to guarantee its protection by trying to keep it confidential. Indeed, some, such as Professor James Rule, a sociologist specializing in research related to privacy and surveillance, have argued that restrictions should be placed on the initial collection of your personal information. Although procedural safeguards are certainly better than nothing, don't let them mislead you. Once your information has been obtained, it is virtually impossible for anyone to give an ironclad assurance about its control or safekeeping. And in this day of high-speed computers, telecommunications, and advanced networks, it is of even greater concern. Beware of those giving assurances of confidentiality—such claims will generally be unsubstantiated.

The next time someone asks you for your personal information, even as little as your address or telephone number, and tells you it will be kept "strictly confidential," ask them what they mean by that. "How will you keep my information confidential?" You might also want to ask them a few more questions: "Who will be allowed to see my information within your organization? Will anyone outside the organization have access to it? Will it be added to any mailing lists without my express consent?"

Two Everyday Scenarios

While you're reading the first scenario below, think of what's wrong with it from a privacy perspective. When we apply Fair Information Practices in the second scenario, you'll see how much they can change the situation. (The name of the relevant FIP will appear in italics in parentheses.)

You go into a store to buy some office supplies. When you go to the cashier to pay, he tells you about a store card you can get that will save you lots of money on various items you buy at the store. Not only is it free, but you can get it by simply filling out an application form. It sounds like a good offer, so you fill out the form. It asks you for the obvious stuff (your name, address, telephone number), but it also asks questions about your business: what type of business it is, how many people it employs, what types of companies you do business with, what your anticipated annual sales are, and on and on for two pages. This makes you a little nervous, because you don't know why you have to provide all this information just to get a discount. When you timidly ask the cashier if they really need all this information, he answers abruptly, "Of course they do, that's why it's on the form. And if you don't fill out the form, you don't get the discount." So, against your better judgment, you fill out the form. But you're uneasy, and you know you'll never return.

When a company follows Fair Information Practices, the situation can be handled much better. Instead of filling out the lengthy form, you take the offensive and tell the cashier you don't like it, as it asks too many irrelevant and personal questions. The cashier says that he's just following company policy, but he tells you that your business is very important to them and he will call their sales manager, Ms. Brown, who is responsible for the information requested on the forms (*accountability*).

You explain to Ms. Brown that you think the form asks for too much confidential information. Though you want to get the discount, you think it should be based on what you buy, not details about your business. Ms. Brown tells you that the information is collected to monitor the purchasing patterns of businesses in order to better serve the needs of their customers. She apologizes that this reason wasn't printed on the form and promises it will appear on the new forms. Ms. Brown goes on to say that it is company policy to tell customers why they are being asked this information and then to use the information only for that purpose (*purpose specification*). She says the company prohibits selling or renting personal information to other companies or exchanging it for mailing-list purposes (*use limitation*). Ms. Brown also tells you that only she and her staff are permitted access to customer profiles. They use a series of computer passwords to ensure that only authorized personnel can enter these files (*security safeguards*). You ask what steps are taken to keep the information up-to-date and accurate (*data quality*). Ms. Brown replies that, while they don't have a quality-control process in place, they encourage customers to review their files whenever they want (*openness, transparency*) and if customers find anything that is wrong or misleading, the company will be glad to correct it (*individual participation; right of access and correction*). You ask whether these policies are written down. Ms. Brown confirms that they are and agrees to make you a copy.

You tell Ms. Brown you are satisfied with everything except one point: you don't think they've narrowed their collection of information to what is really needed for the purpose indicated (*collection limitation*). The two of you review the form and you point out questions you don't want to answer. To her surprise, Ms. Brown agrees that a few of the questions may not be entirely necessary. She says that although she would prefer you to fill them out, she will accept your form without them. You get the promised discount and you leave a satisfied customer.

If you were a customer, which scenario would you prefer? If you were a business, which customer would you prefer?

All of you have experienced some variation of the first scenario, in which you are treated with disdain upon asking a simple question about information someone wants from you. And there is no reason that the second scenario can't become a reality. In fact, some companies are already doing it, volunteering the fact that your information will not be sold or rented.

If you're a businessperson looking for a competitive advantage, start thinking about Fair Information Practices, put them into place, and then tell your customers about them. You will be rewarded not only with their repeat business but also with the business of their family, friends, and business colleagues. You may be surprised at how quickly the word of such respectful and "privacy-friendly" service travels. (Chapter 11 discusses privacy and business practices.)

In these scenarios, we could just as easily have described someone buying clothes or someone buying tools in a hardware store. The same questions can be applied to any company's Fair Information Practices, in any situation where someone is asking for your personal information.

Concluding Thought

Remember that your personal information belongs to you. You own it, no one else. So you should be able to control what information circulates about you. Others (data users) who use your information act only as its custodians. They are entrusted with its care and safekeeping. That's why data users should follow Fair Information Practices. It just makes good sense—good business sense.

Endnotes

1. Spiros Simitis, quoted in David H. Flaherty, *Protecting Privacy in Surveillance Societies* (Chapel Hill: University of North Carolina Press, 1989), p. 377.

2. The complete text of the OECD guidelines may be found in OECD, *Guidelines Governing the Protection of Privacy and Transborder Flows of Personal Data*, 1981, I.L.M. 422, O.E.C.D. Doc. No. C(80) 58 final. They also appear in an appendix to Wayne Madsen, *Handbook of Personal Data Protection* (New York: Stockton Press, 1992), pp. 992–996.

Privacy Laws: Who Has What

Once privacy is invaded, privacy is gone.
U.S. SUPREME COURT JUSTICE WILLIAM O. DOUGLAS

Society has come to realize that privacy is at the heart of liberty in a modern state....Grounded in man's physical and moral autonomy, privacy is essential for the well-being of the individual. For this reason alone, it is worthy of constitutional protection....The restraints imposed on government to pry into the lives of the citizen go to the essence of a democratic state.
SUPREME COURT OF CANADA JUSTICE GÉRARD LA FOREST

A Historical Perspective

In the United States, concern for privacy protection started around the late 1960s, and 1970 saw the passage of the Fair Credit Reporting Act. Although not designed to be a privacy law, this act gives consumers the opportunity to examine their credit files and correct errors. It also places restrictions on the use of information in credit records. Credit-reporting agencies are not permitted to release financial information about individuals except for "legitimate" business needs, such as to establish their creditworthiness. Legitimate business needs, however, can be interpreted very broadly. In addition, although credit-reporting agencies are permitted to share credit information only with employers, insurance companies, and government, and only for a "business transaction involving the consumer," violations are reportedly common. While this act offered some limited protections, they were narrow in scope, contained loopholes, and applied only to credit records.

Several congressional study groups in the late 1960s examined the growing ease with which automated personal information could be gathered and matched with other information. One such group was an advisory committee of the Department of Health, Education, and Welfare (HEW), which in 1973 drafted a Code of Fair Information Practices comprising the following principles:

- There must be no personal data record-keeping systems whose very existence is secret.

- There must be a way for an individual to find out what information about him or her is in a record and how it is used.

- There must be a way for an individual to prevent information about him or her obtained for one purpose from being used or made available for other purposes without consent.

- There must be a way for an individual to correct or amend a record of identifiable information about him or her.

- Any organization using records identifiable to a person must ensure the reliability of the data for their intended use and must take reasonable precautions to prevent misuse of the data.[1]

The work of the U.S. HEW advisory committee led to the passage of the 1974 Privacy Act, which was applicable to federal government records. However, no independent oversight agency—a privacy commissioner or a data protection board—was created. Although the Privacy Act established the Privacy Protection Study Commission in 1974, this was a temporary body with a limited advisory role. The comprehensive report of the commission, *Personal Privacy in an Information Society*, contained some 160 recommendations for improving information practices in both the public and private sectors. The commission's study was far-reaching in its scope, examining such areas as consumer credit records, bank records, mailing lists, insurance records, employment files, medical records, investigative reporting agencies, and school records. The commission's report was released in 1977, but there has been little subsequent activity.

The privacy bill first introduced by Senator Sam Irvin had provided for the creation of a Federal Privacy Board with the sole responsibility of overseeing the law. However, it was eventually deleted in the final round of negotiations leading to the passage of the Privacy Act. In the end, that responsibility was given to the Office of Management and Budget (OMB), an already overextended body. The solution has not proved to be an effective one, as noted by Colin Bennett in his comprehensive work *Regulating Privacy*:

> The American experience has demonstrated, as many have noted, the enormous problems associated with enforcing data protection standards without a commission or some agency whose sole responsibility is privacy. The implementation of the Privacy Act has been inconsistent and sporadic....In the OMB no one official has sole responsibility for Privacy Act enforcement; this office has little incentive to promote data protection when the costs incurred would conflict with its primary mission as the President's expenditure watchdog.[2]

The United States still has no independent oversight body, no watchdog to make sure that the act is being followed, although some efforts have been made in that direction. In 1994 Senator Paul Simon introduced a bill that would have replaced the OMB, as the body overseeing the Privacy Act, with a proposed five-member Data Protection Board. The board would mainly take on an advisory role, helping to guide the private sector in the development of its own privacy codes. Unfortunately, the bill did not come to pass.

Such a form of oversight, possessing primarily advisory powers, can be very effective. Dr. Herbert Burkert, a noted legal expert on data protection, has commented on the value of advisory functions to the success of European data protection agencies: "When conflicts arise, they seem to prefer bargaining to prohibitive measures."[3] The advantages of advisory power is that it facilitates cooperation, communication, and the flow of information into the agency from those being regulated.

While other forms of privacy protection exist in various federal and state laws, they tend to be little known and narrow in their scope. Responding with legislation to isolated concerns as they arise provides a piecemeal approach to a specific problem. The Video Privacy Protection Act of 1988 is a case in point. At the time, Judge Robert Bork was being considered as a nominee for the U.S. Supreme Court. A video rental store that he frequented leaked a list of the judge's video rentals to a newspaper. Although nothing embarrassing was revealed, congressional outrage led to the quick passage of the Video Privacy Protection Act, commonly referred to as the Bork bill. Law professor Joel Reidenberg, an authority on privacy laws, explains that such a "mosaic approach" results from the "American fear of government intervention in private activities and the reluctance to broadly regulate industry. The result of the mosaic is a rather haphazard and unsatisfactory response to each of the privacy concerns."[4]

A number of other industry-specific laws exist in the United States that, while not intended to protect privacy in themselves, do contain some privacy-protective features: the Fair Credit Reporting Act of 1974, the Fair Debt Collection Act of 1977, the Electronic Funds Transfer Act of 1978, the Communications Act of 1984, the Cable Communications Policy Act of 1984, the Electronic Communications Privacy Act of 1986, the Telephone Consumer Protection Act of 1991, and others. Yet despite the appearance of there being a great deal of legislation to protect privacy, there is faint little. Joel Reidenberg notes, "The American legal system does not contain a comprehensive set of privacy rights or principles....The federal constitution does not address privacy for information transactions wholly within the private sector, and state constitutional provisions similarly do not afford rights for private transactions. Instead, legal protection is accorded exclusively through privacy rights created on an ad hoc basis by federal or state legislation or state common law rules."[5]

Four types of common law torts (civil actions) have been developed in state courts to protect against invasions of privacy. You can take civil action against intrusions upon your seclusion, public disclosures of private facts, publicity that presents you in a false light, and the misappropriation of your name or likeness for commercial purposes. Although courts in most states have recognized the majority of these privacy invasions, not all of them are actionable in all states. For example, New York State recognizes only the misappropriation claim, while Minnesota rejects all four rights to privacy.

In Europe, privacy protection started with the work of two international organizations. The Council of Europe began to study the effects of technology on human rights in 1968, recognizing the new threats posed by computer technology that could link and transmit data in ways not widely available before. The council recommended that an instrument be developed to protect personal data held by both the private and public sectors; this ultimately took the form of a resolution to protect individual freedoms by placing limits on the collection, storage, and transmission of personal information, known as Convention 108 (Convention for the Protection of Individuals with Regard to Automatic Processing of Personal Data), and was introduced in 1981.

In 1969, the OECD (Organization for Economic Cooperation and Development) began to examine the implications of "transborder data flow"—that is, personal information leaving a country—on the protection of personal data. In 1980, it developed its internationally recognized Guidelines Governing the Protection of Privacy and Transborder Flows of Personal Data, commonly referred to as the Code of Fair Information Practices.

One of the first privacy laws ever enacted was the Swedish Data Act in 1973, followed by the West German Data Protection Act in 1977 and the French Law on Informatics, Data Banks, and Freedoms in 1978. Each of these countries chose a different method of implementing its laws: the Swedes adopted a licensing system, the Germans established a data protection commissioner, and the French created the National Commission on Informatics and Liberties. While there are numerous differences among these systems, there is one vital similarity: each law includes some means of ensuring that the principles contained in the law are implemented and followed—some method of oversight.

Of the 24 countries in the OECD, 17 have passed some form of privacy legislation. Of the remaining 7 countries, all but one have either introduced bills or had reports prepared by study commissions. With the exception of Turkey, no OECD country has ignored the issue of data protection.[6]

In Canada, a privacy commissioner was established under the Canadian Human Rights Act in 1977. In 1982, the appointment of a privacy commissioner was part of the new Privacy Act. Canada signed the OECD guidelines in 1984 (as did the United States in 1980), committing itself to adhere to those principles. A number of provinces then passed their own privacy laws: Quebec in 1982, Ontario in 1987, Saskatchewan in 1991, British Columbia in 1992, and Alberta in 1994. Each of these provinces has appointed an independent information and privacy commissioner responsible for ensuring compliance with its particular act. The remaining provinces—Manitoba, New Brunswick, Nova Scotia, Newfoundland, and the Northwest Territories—have some form of privacy protection, usually reviewable by the provincial ombudsman or a government official. Prince Edward Island offers no protection.

The provinces that have privacy laws have combined them under one act with freedom of information laws, which give the public the right of access to government documents such as administrative and operational records. The right of access to public records is extremely important in democratic countries: it keeps our governments open and accountable. We should be able to find out how decisions are made and how the government is running our country. This type of information should quite properly be in the public domain, since it is we who vote in our governments, and they who act as our representatives. So we should be able to find out how they're running the country, how they're making decisions about various policies, how much money they're spending, and so forth.

At first glance, the right of access to information and protection of information might seem to be at odds: on the one hand, the goal is to open the door and give people access to information, while on the other, the goal is to close the door and prevent outsiders from getting your information. But these two goals are seldom in conflict, for they apply to two entirely different types of information holdings—one public, one not. Freedom of information applies to the public records of the government, records that are generally *nonpersonal*—that is, not about specific individuals. Privacy protection applies to a different set of records—*personal information*, associated with specific individuals. Public records *should* be accessible to the public; private records *should* be kept private, and used only for the purpose for which they were obtained.

As Marc Rotenberg, law professor and director of the Electronic Privacy Information Center, points out, privacy and access to information are complementary goals, not competing ones. He argues that the view that a balance must be struck between these "competing" interests is basically flawed: "The Congress of 1974 that both adopted the Privacy Act and strengthened the Freedom of Information Act knew better. Private records should be kept private, used only for limited purposes, they said. Public records should be made widely accessible. That there may be overlap between the public and the private does not diminish the essential importance of these principles."[7]

Thus, in our view, there is no inherent conflict in combining freedom of information and protection of privacy into one law. This is the case in a number of Canadian provinces, and it appears to be working very well.

Canada, like the United States, also has a number of sector-specific laws that, while not directed at protecting privacy, offer some limited protection of personal information held by various organizations. Federally, laws that apply to financial institutions are the Bank Act, the Insurance Companies Act, and the Trust and Loan Companies Act. The Telecommunications Act is a federal law overseen by the Canadian Radio-Television and Telecommunications Commission. In addition, some provinces have their respective counterparts such as the Insurance Act, the Loan and Trust Corporations Act, and the Consumer

Reporting Act in Ontario. Enacting specific laws to deal with specific problems is common to both the United States and Canada, but it is an ad hoc, piecemeal approach that fails to provide the full range of protections contained in the Code of Fair Information Practices set out by the OECD.

What Works, What Doesn't

The scope and coverage of privacy laws depend on where you live. In general, data protection laws in Europe cover the private sector as well as the public sector. There, privacy laws apply not only to government operations but also to private enterprise and commercial transactions. In North America, however, privacy laws (except in Quebec) apply only to the public sector, not to the private sector. (There are a few limited exceptions to this, such as the Consumer Credit Reporting Act and the Telecommunications Act in Canada, which extend certain privacy principles to the respective private sector industries, but these were never intended to serve as privacy-protection laws, nor may decisions arising out of them be appealed to a privacy commissioner.) This leaves you with little judicial recourse when it comes to privacy complaints involving businesses or organizations not covered by these laws.

Voluntary Privacy Codes

A number of companies, though, seeing the writing on the wall, have voluntarily developed their own privacy codes of conduct. American Express, Equifax, the Information Industry Association of America, Stentor, the Direct Marketing Association (DMA) and the Canadian DMA, the Canadian Bankers Association, and the Insurance Bureau of Canada, to name a few, have all introduced privacy codes, loosely modeled on the OECD's Fair Information Practices. Needless to say, self-regulation is much more palatable to these organizations than government regulation, and a number of industry-led codes have undoubtedly been adopted to preempt legislation.

A voluntary privacy code is certainly preferable to no self-regulation. But such codes have a number of inherent problems. First, since they are voluntary in nature, there is nothing to compel member companies to abide by them. Second, there is little recourse that you, the consumer, have if you want to complain. You can complain, of course, but without some independent body to oversee the company's information practices, you may get no satisfaction whatsoever, and there's no one else to appeal to.

A study of voluntary codes undertaken by the Public Interest Advocacy Center found that such codes suffered from the following problems:

- A conflict of interest in underinclusion of consumers in the code development and code administration process
- Inadequate code coverage
- Low consumer awareness of issues and of code provisions
- Lack of adequate sanctions
- General lack of systematic procedures to measure or monitor compliance
- In the few cases where formal monitoring studies have been conducted, evidence of low levels of compliance.[8]

Despite these negative findings, the study did not recommend eliminating sector-specific codes, because of their key strength over broad legislation—their ability to address specific issues in a particular sector. Any standards developed could be tailor-made to the situation, making them more focused and more relevant.

While privacy laws are generally regarded as being superior to self-regulating voluntary codes, they are not without their problems. Some scholars argue that the presence of privacy laws and oversight commissions breeds a degree of complacency, which over time may create a false sense of security about data protection. After his comprehensive review of the privacy protection laws and oversight authorities in five countries, Privacy Commissioner David Flaherty concluded:

> How will data protection authorities look by the year 2000? There is a real risk that they will be looked back upon as a rather quaint, failed effort to cope with an overpowering technological tide rather than as a fruitful, successful exercise in promoting the coexistence of competing human and social values....As an optimist and an overall admirer of their track record to date, it is my judgment that the existing model of having a data protection agency to articulate privacy interests on a continuing basis will have long-term validity for the control of surveillance.[9]

Despite identifying a number of problems with existing privacy laws and the independent agencies that oversee them, Flaherty states that their success at limiting surveillance is extensive. "They have reduced the risks of the actual 'death of privacy' or the 'end of private life.'...In essence, data protection commissioners or agencies are an alarm system for the protection of privacy."[10] Others agree. Marc Rotenberg of the Electronic Privacy Information Center argues that even with good privacy laws, little protection is provided without adequate oversight. He says the U.S. Privacy Act "failed to deliver....The absence of effective oversight, the lack of significant incentives to limit violations, and the exceptions carved out for law enforcement are just a few of the problems we face today with our current privacy law for government records."[11]

The best solution may be one that combines a privacy law, overseen by an independent privacy commission, with sector-specific codes that complement the law. Such a model exists in several countries, such as the Netherlands and New Zealand, where codes of practice are being negotiated sector by sector and blended with the central law, which serves as the minimum standard. Such an arrangement provides individual sectors with the advantage of specific, detailed applications of the broad statutory provisions of the law, while preserving the benefits of a legislative framework.

The European Union: How It Could Affect You

One reason we should all be paying some attention to these matters is the European Union's Directive on Data Protection, an attempt to harmonize the data protection laws of the 12 member countries of the EU. The 1990 draft directive on "the protection of individuals with regard to the processing of personal data and on the free movement of such data" would establish a minimum standard by which member countries would have to abide. What is important to those outside the EU is that the directive would prohibit the transfer of personal information to nonmember countries that lacked "equivalent" data protection—an attempt to regulate transborder data flows of personal information.

The draft directive was revised in 1992 to allow greater flexibility on a variety of issues and to reduce the level of data protection required in nonmember countries from "equivalent" to "adequate." A determination of adequacy will be based on "the nature of the data, the purpose and duration of the processing, the legislative provisions, both general and sectoral...and the professional rules which are complied with in that country." Nonetheless, the prohibition on transfers of personal information to nonmember countries lacking "adequate protection" is subject to only limited exceptions:

- The data subject consents to the transfer and has been informed of the recipient country's inadequate level of protection.
- The transfer is necessary for the performance of a contract.
- The transfer is necessary on important public interest grounds, or to protect the vital interests of the data subject.

If we in North America are not careful, the EU directive could present us with a formidable noneconomic trade barrier. The directive, which was formally approved and adopted by the Council of Ministers on July 24, 1995, has already created a strong incentive for the private sector in North America to get its proverbial "act together" with respect to data protection.

Companies wishing to continue to do business with Europe have realized that the existing inadequate state of data protection will not meet the requirements of the EU directive. Nor, for that matter, will it ultimately meet the requirements of American and Canadian citizens. As a result, various businesses and industries have started to develop voluntary industrywide privacy codes. (Some of these codes will be discussed in Chapter 11.)

Concluding Thought

A voluntary privacy code is better than nothing. A privacy law is better than a voluntary code. A law and a sector-specific privacy code is even better. But a law without an independent body to make sure the law is being followed may only serve as window dressing: "It is not enough to simply pass a data protection law...an agency charged with its implementation is essential to make the law work in practice."[12]

Endnotes

1. Summarized from *Records, Computers, and the Rights of Citizens*, Report of the Secretary's Advisory Committee on Automated Personal Data Systems (Washington, D.C.: Department of Health, Education, and Welfare, 1973).

2. Colin J. Bennett, *Regulating Privacy: Data Protection and Public Policy in Europe and the United States* (New York: Cornell University Press, 1992), p. 241.

3. Herbert Burkert, "Institutions of Data Protection: An Attempt at a Functional Explanation of European Data Protection Laws," *Computer Law Journal*, Vol. 3: (1981): 181–188.

4. Joel R. Reidenberg, "Privacy in the Information Economy: A Fortress or Frontier for Individual Rights?" Federal Communications Law Journal, Vol. 44, No. 2 (1993), p. 209.

5. Reidenberg, "Privacy in the Information Economy," p. 208.

6. Bennett, *Regulating Privacy: Data Protection and Public Policy in Europe and the United States,* p. 56.

7. Marc Rotenberg, "Privacy Protection," *Government Information Quarterly,* Vol. 11, No. 3 (1994), p. 254.

8. Lola Fabowale, *Voluntary Codes: A Viable Alternative to Government Legislation?* (Ottawa: Public Interest Advocacy Center, May 1994), p. 80.

9. David H. Flaherty, *Protecting Privacy in Surveillance Societies* (Chapel Hill: University of North Carolina Press, 1989), pp. 406–407.

10. Flaherty, *Protecting Privacy,* p. 383.

11. Rotenberg, "Privacy Protection," p. 253.

12. Flaherty, *Protecting Privacy,* p. 380.

The Growth of Computers... the Rise of Surveillance

If—or is it when?—computers are permitted to talk to one another, when they are interlinked, they can spew out a roomful of data on each of us that will leave us naked before whoever gains access to the information....But we must be vigilant against their misuse, either accidentally or intentionally. WALTER CRONKITE, 1980

Threats to privacy certainly existed in precomputer times, but they were far less of a concern. Then, if you wanted to pry into someone's information, you had to go to a lot of trouble. In an entirely paper-based world, you would have to physically travel to each place where that person's files were and review each piece of paper in each file. Such detective work would have required a lot of time and money.

With the advent of powerful computers and high-speed networks, the electronic monitoring and tracking of people's activities has become not only easy, but desirable—not to the individual, but to the ever-growing number of people wanting to know more and more about the individual. Surveillance began to take on a new meaning:

> Computerization is robbing individuals of the ability to monitor and control the ways information about them is used....The foundation is being laid for a dossier society, in which computers could be used to infer individuals' lifestyles, habits, whereabouts, and associations from data collected in ordinary consumer transactions....As computerization becomes more pervasive, the potential for these problems will grow dramatically.[1]

The Deadly Duo

Coupled with the growth of computers and networked communications has been the growth of large organizations, both public and private, and their bureaucracies. It appears that bureaucracies have an insatiable desire for information. This urge to know everything about the people they "serve" was satisfied by the computer's ability to electronically link diverse databases of information relating to the same individual. Thus, vast amounts of personal information could be compiled fairly easily.

As organizations grew larger and computerization became more pervasive, the potential for surveillance grew dramatically. Not only could information be easily compiled and stored but the data-linking abilities of computers could create personal profiles about individuals. Some have referred to this as the development of "dossiers," electronic dossiers or files on potentially everyone, leading ultimately to a surveillance society. Others have called this process "dataveillance," characterized by *how* these profiles are compiled—through data linked electronically from diverse databases containing vast amounts of personal information.

Surveillance: Orwell Didn't Know the Half of It

George Orwell captured the watchful eye of the state over its citizens in his classic work *Nineteen Eighty-Four,* written in 1948. Orwell portrayed a futuristic society in which surveillance by the state was the norm, not the exception. Big Brother peered into each and every home and workplace through giant telescreens; there was virtually nowhere to escape from the intrusive gaze of his watchful eye; nowhere to be free from intrusion or interruption; nowhere to be free. Complete and total surveillance—from the outside. But Orwell didn't know about present-day computers and the ever-growing maze of telecommunication networks.

Orwell was not the first to write about surveillance. Jeremy Bentham wrote about his Panopticon, or "all-seeing place," in 1791. But as Professor David Lyon notes in *The Electronic*

Eye: The Rise of Surveillance Society, Bentham viewed surveillance as a necessary good, not an evil. Whereas Orwell viewed surveillance as being undesirable and depicted it as such (a dystopia), Bentham welcomed it in the context of a prison. He developed an ingenious model of prison surveillance based on the *illusion* of surveillance. Control was asserted through the prisoners' *belief* that they were constantly being watched. Since the prisoners had no means of actually knowing, they had to assume the worst.

What Orwell and Bentham didn't envision was another form of surveillance, perhaps more intrusive than physical surveillance (through cameras and prison guards), and that is surveillance from the inside, "little brother," lurking in the digital world of computers and networks. In the world of so-called cyberspace, we may have more to fear than from conventional forms of external surveillance.

Cyberspace: The Home of Little Brother

Cyberspace is the electronic airways and information residing in electronic or digital form, capable of being transmitted online via networked communications. Novelist William Gibson coined this term, referring to it as "lines of nonlight...the total data on all the networked computers in the world." What it enables people to do can be chilling. That's where "little brother" comes in—a far more powerful and, some would argue, more effective form of intrusive surveillance. Electronic surveillance may be more powerful than the type of physical surveillance (watching, listening) envisioned by Orwell in that it is invisible, as were the ever-watchful eyes in Bentham's model. And most people don't know about the existence of electronic surveillance; they don't know that they're being robbed of their privacy. And if you don't believe how much information about you can be found through the push of a few computer keys or the click of a mouse, think again. In *Privacy for Sale,* Jeffrey Rothfeder chronicles a seemingly endless array of databases that anyone with a computer, a modem, and a little know-how can gain easy access to.

Monitoring and tracking your movements, transactions, and communications (referred to as transaction-generated information) with this inner form of surveillance may indeed be more insidious than the surveillance envisioned by Orwell. In the world of Big Brother, the fact of being watched could not be escaped; its existence was abundantly clear to all. In today's world, however, this is seldom the case. With massive data collection and computer linkages of diverse databases, little may remain private, but the invisible nature of much of this activity makes it more insidious, because you don't know it's taking place. In *Undercover*, Professor Gary Marx skillfully analyzes how this electronic or "new surveillance" is more extensive, decentralized, involuntary, and invisible (or of lesser visibility). The invisible nature of this activity heightens the capacity for surveillance and the gradual but steady erosion of your privacy.

In "Information Technology and Dataveillance," Australia's Roger Clarke argues that surveillance through the use of data is now "supplanting conventional surveillance techniques."[2] Clarke defines dataveillance as the systematic use of personal data, residing in electronic databases, in the investigation or monitoring of the actions or communications of one or more people. He considers dataveillance to be technically and economically superior to traditional forms of surveillance.

Historically, privacy advocates have feared the creation of one vast, centralized computer database containing massive amounts of information—the "Fort Knox" of personal information, needing to be guarded vigorously, around the clock. However, with the advent of lightning-speed networks, the Fort Knox model of centralized dossiers need not materialize. It is no longer necessary because multiple databases scattered across the world can now be easily linked to create a comprehensive profile. As Clarke notes, all that is required is a range of personal databases, linked by telecommunications networks, and a consistent method of identification (such as a health insurance or social security number).

The threat posed by dataveillance lies in how all the different pieces of information about you, stored in numerous databases, can be merged, sorted, and analyzed to create a personal profile, or data image, of you. It is possible not only to track your activities but also to sketch a fairly accurate picture of you and your habits, enabling others to "know" you without ever knowing you, and without you ever knowing.

You might well wonder where all the information stored in these databases comes from, because you don't recall giving away any personal information. Well have you ever done any of the following: bought a car, rented an apartment, bought a suit, bought a book, bought something at the supermarket, bought an airline ticket, reserved a hotel room, ordered underwear from a mail-order catalog, joined a book club, used a telephone, used an automated teller, opened a bank account, ordered a pizza, rented a video, filled out a product warranty card, subscribed to a magazine, applied for a government program, applied for a job, applied for a loan, applied for insurance, gone to the hospital, had a baby, had a blood test, had a prescription filled? Each of these transactions can lead to an electronic record being created in a database somewhere, leaving a permanent data trail of your preferences, habits, and activities.

Every day, people unknowingly provide unnecessary personal information and unwittingly feed the growth of dataveillance by allowing outsiders into their lives. Such newspaper headlines as "Your Supermarket Knows Who You Are...Grocery Store Keeps Tabs on Customers" illustrate the extent of information gathering by enterprises as unlikely as grocery stores. (Remember the checkout scanners and your grocery store savings card?) And with the existing electronic web of networks and the impending arrival of the information highway, all the information contained in these databases can be brought together to construct a very clear and, one hopes, accurate picture of you.

The Chilling Effect of Errors

While it is preferable, from a privacy perspective, that no data picture be taken, if one must exist, pray that it is an accurate one, and that the right information is linked to you. Otherwise, misfortune may fall upon you. This is no exaggeration, as the following example cited by Jeffrey Rothfedder illustrates. James Russell Wiggins, a father of four, applied for and got a $70,000 sales position with a cable company in Washington, D.C. A routine preemployment background check, however, revealed that Wiggins had been convicted of possessing cocaine. The next day, he was fired. Wiggins' employer felt justified in firing him, not only because he had a previous criminal record but because he had concealed this fact from the company. Wiggins was completely shocked; he denied ever having a criminal record.

It turned out that the credit bureau hired to conduct the background check had mistakenly pulled the criminal record of a James Ray Wiggins, not James Russell Wiggins, and the error went undetected even though the two men had different middle names, birthdates, addresses, and social security numbers. Even after the explanation was found, however, Wiggins didn't get his job back.

Very often, such mistakes may never be revealed. If the background check had been done before Wiggins was hired, he simply wouldn't have been hired, and he wouldn't have known why. Moreover, from that point on, lingering in some database, a criminal conviction for possession of cocaine would be linked with his name, virtually eliminating his chances of ever getting a good job—again without his ever knowing why. This is one good reason that the right of access to your personal information is so important.

The problem of errors is compounded with the secondary uses of your information. Janlori Goldman, a lawyer formerly with the American Civil Liberties Union and now with the Center for Democracy and Technology, cautioned, "There's barely a piece of information about people that isn't used for far different purposes than it was initially gathered for, and always without their approval."[3] The likelihood of ever finding all the instances of secondary use and locating the myriad places where your information might be stored, to check it for accuracy, is becoming exceedingly remote. Caution must be taken in the first instance.

Large databases especially are notorious for their error rates—estimates range from 20 to 30 percent. Not comforting news, especially when a wide range of the decisions being made in such areas as employment, insurance, credit, and accommodations rely on information obtained from these databases. Employers are becoming more and more data-driven, seeking as much information as they can get about potential employees. Preemployment background checks have become big business. And if employees, for instance, don't know what's being said about them in the information an employer receives, they are already at a distinct disadvantage, more so if the information happens to be wrong. The individual doesn't stand a chance; since you don't know about the error, you won't be able do anything to correct it.

Personal Profiles

Developing mailing lists for marketing purposes has turned into a fine art through such techniques as segmenting, targeting, and micromarketing. Instead of mailing a solicitation to thousands of people at random, it is far better to target the particular market desired, as specifically as possible. And this is where detailed personal profiles are highly desirable to marketers.

With refined demographics (lives in a middle-class neighborhood; income is $40,000), overlayed onto specific shopping preferences (bought a Ford minivan; owns a Burberry raincoat) and lifestyle indicators (joined a gym; went to a spa), it isn't hard to create an individual profile. And there's a huge business for data bankers who rent out lists to promotion-hungry companies. No wonder Americans receive close to 63 billion pieces of junk mail and 20 billion unsolicited telemarketing calls every year.

A wide range of lists abound. Some are fairly general— birthday lists, turning-point age lists (18, 21, 30, 40, 50), height and weight lists, and lists on coupon clippers, cosmetics buyers, or weight-conscious consumers. Other lists are far more specific—beer drinkers, male buyers of fashion underwear, married "adult video enthusiasts," antitax donators, retired military personnel, conservative Republican donors, impotent middle-aged men, and gay and lesbian hotel guests. As one target market specialist said, "Tell me someone's zip code and I can predict what they eat, drink, drive—even think."

If the private sector followed the use limitation principle of the Code of Fair Information Practices, there would be virtually no such data linkage or personal profiling without your knowledge or consent, because almost all these activities consist of secondary uses of your personal information: your information is being used beyond the primary purpose for which it was collected. Nor are you, the data subject, informed of the secondary uses of your information, as the purpose specification principle requires. Therefore, if Fair Information Practices were followed by both government and private enterprises, there would be little electronic surveillance of your activities (without your knowing about it).

The time to change these practices is now. As the networking capabilities of technology increase, these activities will become easier and more common. Yet we must resist the temptation to blame technology. Technology itself is neutral, value-free. It is the *uses* of technology that lead to encroachments on personal privacy. If we must blame someone, we must blame ourselves, in part, for the abuses of technology. You may not like the amount of personal information about you being amassed, but unless you speak up and challenge the practice, you are silently supporting it.

Computer Matching

A procedure that government organizations commonly use is *computer matching*—the electronic comparison of two or more databases containing personal information, a form of "mass" dataveillance. The object is to screen groups of people to find those worth subjecting to personal dataveillance. Since the individuals warranting investigation are unknown at the beginning of the computer match, the practice is often likened to a "fishing expedition."

Computer matching is used for a variety of purposes, primarily detecting fraud, recouping debts, and verifying continuing eligibility for government programs. If, for example, Alan Bacon was collecting unemployment insurance, then his name should not appear on a list of government employees. Or if Jane Preston is due to receive an income tax refund of $985, then she should have sufficient funds to pay off the amount owing on her government student loan of $855. A comparison of the databases containing income tax refunds and student loans outstanding would yield a list of "hits" of names that appeared on both. The names of those appearing on this "hit list" would have met the criteria selected for the computer match.

So what could be wrong with such a laudable effort to reduce fraud and abuse of the system? To begin with, the cost-cutting claims of computer matching have been generally unsubstantiated. A 1986 study by the U.S. Office of Technology Assessment found that "no firm evidence is available to determine the costs and benefits of computer matching and to document claims...that computer matching is cost-effective." Further, computer matching that takes place without proper verification of the information yielded from the match is not only a denial of due process but often just plain wrong. A "raw hit," or unverified information (about a suspected individual) yielded from a match can lead to the end of benefits or entitlement to a program without the person being given an opportunity to challenge the decision or offer evidence to the contrary. Principles of due process require that you be given the opportunity to challenge your accuser before a decision against you is made. In this case, it would involve your right to refute the government's records prior to benefits being cut off or your tax refund being withheld.

Basing decisions that adversely affect data subjects solely on raw hits also violates another fundamental principle of democratic societies—the presumption of innocence. People singled out by raw hits are not presumed to be innocent until proved guilty; they are treated as if they are guilty from the start. They are not given the opportunity to defend themselves before a decision is made that might affect them detrimentally.

Garbage In, Garbage Out

Another major problem with computer matching is with the accuracy of the yielded information. This will only be as good as the accuracy of the information contained in the databases used in the match, which may be fraught with errors. A comprehensive report titled *Privacy and Computer Matching* highlights the questionable quality and accuracy of information: "There is considerable concern over the ability of computer matches to produce accurate and reliable results....Errors result from erroneously reported or inaccurately entered data, time lags, hardware and software problems, and the abstract nature of the decision process."

The problem is compounded when incorrect information from a match is later used elsewhere, and then forms part of another database, which in turn may be used in a subsequent match—reproducing the error again and again. By that time, the data subject has lost all control over this information and has no chance of setting the record straight.

Once you build in the necessary protections to ensure the right of due process and introduce safeguards to allow some measure of accuracy and security, for both the information used and the information yielded from computer matches, the cost-effectiveness of such matches becomes questionable. This is why it is always advisable to start with a cost-benefit analysis to assess whether there is some other way to obtain the desired information that is also more protective of privacy.

In the face of such problems, a number of jurisdictions have introduced legislation or policies to regulate computer matching. The United States passed the Computer Matching and Privacy Protection Act in 1988 to ensure that all individuals involved in a match were given due process and to establish uniform procedures by which matches would be conducted. This law also established several oversight mechanisms. In 1989, the Canadian government introduced a policy titled Data Matching and Control of the Social Insurance Number. Similar to the American law, it required that the public be notified of a proposed match and that safeguards be in place to ensure the security of the information relating to suspected individuals. A cost-benefit analysis also had to be conducted to determine whether there were more cost-effective ways than computer matches to detect fraud or identify violators. An assessment containing the purpose, the legal authority, a cost-benefit analysis, and other details of the proposed computer match must be submitted to data integrity boards in the United States, or to the privacy commissioner in Canada.

Although these policies may sound good on paper, their effectiveness in practice is questionable. Under the present scheme, there is no way to compel federal Canadian agencies to submit such assessments to the privacy commissioner. (In 1993, only 18 assessments were submitted.) U.S. data integrity boards are internal forms of review (whereas Canada's is external), consisting of senior officials from within the same government agency that is proposing the computer match. There is obviously little independence in this form of oversight and little incentive not to approve matches.

A 1993 report prepared by the U.S. General Accounting Office (GAO) on how government agencies were implementing the computer-matching law was entitled *Computer Matching: Quality of Decisions and Supporting Analyses Little Affected by 1988 Act*. The findings of the study were not encouraging. The quality of the cost-benefit analyses conducted to justify computer matches was found to be very weak. Estimates of costs, benefits, or both were either entirely missing or unsupported. Perhaps more troubling was the finding that not one computer match had ever been canceled or turned down as a result of the review process. Nor did the GAO find any evidence that the requirements of the act were used to determine whether a match should be approved. This is further evidence that a law by itself, without independent oversight, is not enough.

France and Germany have more restrictive data protection laws that better address the problems associated with computer matching. In France, the National Commission on Informatics and Liberties must authorize all data linkages by controlling applications for processing identifiable data. The commission is generally opposed to linkages on the principle that data should be used only for the purpose for which it was collected. The German Federal Data Protection Act contains a general prohibition, applicable to all public bodies and agencies, against the disclosure of personal data from one agency to another. With the passing of the European Union's Directive on Data Protection, there will be considerable harmonization in the data processing practices of member countries. Apart from the general provisions requiring adherence to Fair Information Practices, the directive contains a clause that explicitly addresses the issue of "automated individual decisions": "Member states shall grant the right to every person not to be subjected to an administrative or private decision adversely affecting him which is based solely on automatic processing defining a personality profile." Clearly, computerized data linkages will increasingly be looked upon with disfavor.

Concluding Thought

Once your personal information has been obtained (either directly from you or indirectly from hundreds of sources) and is entered into a database, it is virtually impossible to stem the flow of that information—to stop others from using it. It is being gathered; personal profiles are being developed. The marketing opportunities are endless. So be careful how much of your highly sought after information you give away.

Endnotes

1. David Chaum, "Security Without Identification: Transaction Systems to Make Big Brother Obsolete," *Journal for the Association of Computing Machinery*, Vol. 28, No. 10 (October 1985), p. 1030.

2. Roger A. Clarke, "Information Technology and Dataveillance," *Communications of the ACM*, Vol. 31, No. 5 (May 1988): p. 499.

3. Janlori Goldman, quoted in Jeffrey Rothfeder, *Privacy for Sale: How Computerization Has Made Everyone's Private Life an Open Secret* (New York: Simon & Schuster, 1992), p. 25.

THE REAL-LIFE
SPINOUT

The Information Highway: The Road Well Traveled?

Someone is always watching. Your wake-up call, overnight messages, and personalized news summary come from the database of your local telephone exchange. The brand of coffee you gulp for breakfast, like all your purchases, was recorded when you paid with your charge card. Your televiewing habits are monitored by the same cable-TV firm that offers you 500 channels. Your drive to work is recorded by the traffic-monitoring system...the swipe of a security card lets you into your office, where your movements and telephone conversations are recorded via the tiny phone-computer on your wrist. The date is August 7th 2003.

The Economist, 1993

Up to this point, we have traced the path of technology through the growth of computers, the development of networks and telecommunications, and the growth of large organizations and their bureaucracies, all of which have led to the rise of surveillance activities. We have also traced the development of Fair Information Practices and privacy laws. Nowhere will these be needed more than now—at the design stage of the information highway. Construction is about to begin.

Fact or Fiction: What Is It?

Everyone wants to know what the I-way will be like. Everyone in book publishing, television making, newspaper selling, telephone providing, and satellite broadcasting would like to know how it will affect his or her livelihood. Could some expert please tell them what to back, what to expect?...But there is an expert vacuum.   —Editor, *Wired Magazine*

There may never have been so much talk about an unknown entity as there has been about the information highway. There has already been a great deal of debate over the name of this yet-to-be-determined phenomenon. The top contenders appear to be: the information highway, the information super-highway, the electronic highway, the infocosm, the infobahn (after the German autobahn, or pathway), the agora (after the Greek word for marketplace), and simply the I-way. We will refer to it as the information highway or, at times, simply the highway.

Nor have there been as many definitions about an unknown entity as have appeared for the information high-way—and well before much electronic concrete has been laid. The convergence of voice (telephone), video (television), and data (computing) is a key component of the promised highway. Some refer to the highway as a seamless network of net-works—a worldwide information and communications infra-structure that will greatly facilitate the exchange of informa-tion and two-way interactive services. With a device referred to as an "appliance," much like the cable converter box that sits on top of your television set, your TV or computer will become transformed into one interactive telephone/TV/computer that will transmit signals via networked communications into your home, your workplace, your hotel room—wherever you may find yourself with electronic access. Companies are already unveiling such products as the "ultimate home appliance," consisting of six devices wrapped into one: the television, per-sonal computer, telephone, answering machine, fax machine, and CD. Many others will follow.

The Best and the Worst

The words of Charles Dickens cogently capture our view of the emerging highway: "It was the best of times...it was the worst of times." Perhaps this will be the tale of two paths, each going in opposite directions. The highway promises to promote economic development and to dramatically change the way societies create wealth, but it also has its dark side. Recent works such as Clifford Stoll's *Silicon Snake Oil* question the social impact of networks like the Internet. Information specialist Tom Riley says that fears about the new technologies extend well beyond paranoia: "It is wise to sound a note of caution about information technologies which on one side, can hold the promise for a brave new world whose society is far more controlled and despotic than Orwell ever imagined."[1] But let's look at the promise of the highway first.

As government programs become deliverable electronically, government itself will be reinvented. "Virtual" government agencies, for example, providing social benefits or entitlements can eliminate the frustration and inefficiencies of dealing with half a dozen different agencies. The new networks will help create new kinds of firms and institutions, shifting from the old command-and-control hierarchy to networked, team-based structures. The technology promises to radically alter the kind of work many of us do.

Multimedia systems capable of delivering many separate functions at once are more effective than their data processing predecessors, enabling the creation of "wholistic jobs" rather than the piecemeal work systems of the past. Students will have access to the best authorities around the world, freeing up teachers to give individual attention and become coaches rather than instructors. Health care will become integrated, ensuring that patients can be treated as people, not just the sum of their parts. Doctors will be able to collaborate from around the world and from remote locations, seeing on their computer screens such things as the malformed heart of an infant before and during a life-saving operation.

The convenience of this electronic marvel will be extensive. You will be able to do all your banking on the highway, your shopping, your movie viewing. You'll have access to a wide range of government and business services, be able to order a pizza, shop for groceries, order your prescriptions, accomplish your work, videoconference with anyone around the world—the list goes on and on. And all this from something we're not really sure of. But we know it's coming.

Yet the information highway will not be used solely as a commercial medium for selling and shopping or as an entertainment medium. Some hope that it will be used primarily for educational purposes as a vehicle for information exchange. Not only will information become the principal form of exchange on the highway, it will also be the main by-product. Because of the highway's two-way interactive nature, people will ride it as both information users/consumers and information providers. The gap between users and providers is closing.

When the information involved is not private or confidential, any medium that facilitates its exchange and makes it widely available is welcome. Access to government records, library holdings, research materials, and mountains of other public information could be yours at a keystroke. But we must guard against the creation of distinct groups of information haves and have-nots and the emergence of an information elite.

Universal access, affordability, and openness are key. Access to information should be available equally to all, regardless of location or other impediments, and at a reasonable cost. By open, we mean that the highway must allow for "interoperability," or permit connections among different systems, so that no one information carrier can put up technological roadblocks to give itself an advantage in the marketplace. We believe that every effort must be made to avoid information elitism on the highway, to ensure that the benefits of access to information are shared with all those who wish to avail themselves of the service.

Who will ensure that the principles of universal access, affordability, and openness are maintained on the highway? What will be the regulatory balance among government, the private sector, and self-regulating individuals? Many people would like to keep government's involvement to a minimum, but without some government regulation and intervention, commercial interests would have little regard for these principles, or for your privacy. As Ken Auletta wrote in *The New Yorker* (January 17, 1994), "To sell advertising, communications companies will naturally want to sell information that citizens would rather keep private. Who, if not government, would protect citizens from what has been called data rape?...If government does not at times intercede as a referee, it leaves the very success of the information superhighway at risk."

For the highway to be successful, it must be widely accepted and used. For it to be widely accepted and used, the public must have confidence that the highway will not trample their rights or jeopardize their privacy. Yet too many questions remain unanswered. What protections, if any, will apply to the bits of information that travel the highway? Will users be able to select the level of security they wish for the information they transmit? Will there be rules to direct the traffic? Will there be traffic cops to enforce those rules, or will the rules be cast aside as being unenforceable? It seems that government must play a leading role in designing and overseeing the information highway.

Some have warned that the rules of conduct now found in legislation will not be sufficient to protect our privacy on the highway. The traditional approach to such things as intellectual property and copyright may have to be entirely rethought, and amending our existing laws may not be enough. In *Being Digital,* Nicholas Negroponte, founder and director of the MIT Media Lab, says that "copyright is totally out of date. It is a Gutenberg artifact. Since it is a reactive process, it will probably have to break down completely before it is corrected."[2] And Paul Hoffert, director of the CulTech research group, believes that "the problems posed by the new technology are insoluble within the current legal framework. We will have to find solutions outside of legislation."[3] They're right. Certainly some of the solutions that will be needed to protect privacy in the year 2000 will not be found in legislation.

The Internet: The Ultimate

Given that little is clear about the construction of the information highway, it should come as no surprise that considerable debate surrounds what role an existing worldwide network, the Internet, will play in these developments. One option is that instead of building entirely new communications networks, we could build upon existing ones such as the expansive Internet or the "Net," which links hundreds of networks around the world in a seemingly endless electronic maze. The Net was built more than a quarter century ago by the U.S. armed forces to maintain communications in the event of such things as nuclear war. Today the Net has an estimated 32 million users (spread over 130 countries), and is growing at a rate of roughly 10 percent a month.

The Net is packed with thousands of databases, personal mailboxes, and public electronic forums that take the form of bulletin boards and Usenet news groups. The topics up for discussion are as extensive as the number of groups, ranging from the intricacies of physics and chaos theory to enticing "alt" or alternative groups for the not so shy. Not only does the Net give you access to huge amounts of information on just about any subject, it also provides a relatively inexpensive and efficient means of communication. Electronic mail, or e-mail, on the Net also allows you to talk with anyone anywhere in the world for a fraction of the cost of a long-distance phone call. Also, you can transmit or receive as much text as you wish, again without any specific charges for its transmission.

Not that long ago, the Internet was the exclusive domain of the academic community—researchers, scientists, professors, and university students. In recent years, though, businesses, consumers, and just plain folk have been flooding onto the Net, exchanging information and exploring the untapped sources of commerce waiting in the wings. (Commercial solicitation on the Net used to be unwelcome, and advertising was informally banned. But that appears to be changing. In 1994 the Home Shopping Network, the prominent U.S. television retailer, purchased the rights to electronic shopping on the Net.)

Online Service Providers

Growth in the secondary uses of your personal information may come from online service providers—companies that provide you with access to the Internet as well as other information services. The largest of such companies are probably well-known to you: CompuServe, America Online and Prodigy, to name a few. These service providers are growing at a fast pace. And every time someone signs up with them, they receive a wealth of personal information, information ripe for sale as customer lists to marketing companies.

Once the sale of such information started getting the attention of the media, a number of users and politicians objected to the practice. As a result of the ensuing pressure, companies such as America Online added an opt-out clause permitting users to say no to having their information sold to marketers. But is this enough? Are most users aware of this option or, in its absence, the secondary uses that will be made of their personal information? Probably not.

You can be sure that marketers will want access to the millions of online users available through service providers' mailing lists. Before they can pitch specific products, though, they must first get a sense of users' tastes and personal preferences. But this shouldn't take too long; a number of firms are creating software programs to capture where Net users are browsing and what they are viewing, reading, and buying. Take, for example, Venture Communications Electronic Marketing Inc. of New York, which is pitching a "free offer" service through CompuServe and Prodigy. On a weekly basis, Venture's computer sifts through the people who accepted its free offers and passes along their names, addresses, and telephone numbers to company sponsors. These lists may also be rented to other businesses for subsequent marketing efforts. As always, beware of free offers.

One company, however, has chosen to take a different approach. "Microsoft, the giant software company based in Redmond, Washington, stunned the business world when it announced in late July that it would not sell data about customers to its soon-to-be unveiled Microsoft Network (MSN)."[4] Not without their express consent, anyway: "It will begin by asking customers up front whether or not they want to be solicited—in effect, an opt-in."[5] (See Chapter 7 for a discussion of the benefits of opt-in over opt-out.) The marketing director for MSN, Bill Miller, said that customers should be permitted to make this choice right from the beginning when they sign up for the service. They should also be able to get themselves off the list, easily, at a later time. Further, if someday you decide to leave MSN, your name and information will be deleted from Microsoft's database. Miller was quoted as saying, "It gives some control and protects the people to whom the information really belongs—the customers—to a much greater degree than has ever existed in direct marketing in the United States."[6]

Microsoft's privacy policy is progressive compared with others in the industry. But this should come as no surprise. Bill Gates, the head of Microsoft, appears to be concerned about his privacy in an increasingly networked world. In a column in *The New York Times,* Gates wrote an article called "Privacy: Who Should Know What About Whom." He started by saying, "If you're worried about threats to privacy in the emerging electronic age, you're not alone. I'm worried too." He went on to discuss the threats posed by networks in sharing and pooling information about your personal preferences, developing an electronic profile of you in the process. "Privacy is in peril if the information spreads too far or is pooled too widely or is collected without your consent." Bill Gates feels that the development of public policy is critical: "Public policy is needed. I expect privacy to be heavily debated and thoughtful policies to emerge. These new policies will extend the privacy laws that are already on the books in many countries."[7] One can only hope that this will take place.

The Federal Trade Commission (FTC) has also taken an interest in privacy and other consumer issues in cyberspace. The FTC held a 2-day meeting in April 1995 to examine these issues in the context of the Global Information Infrastructure. On September 7, the FTC announced its intention to develop self-regulatory privacy principles for online spaces, including the Internet. The FTC also held a 4-day session on the "Emerging High-Tech Global Marketplace" in November: half a day was devoted to the question of online privacy. Commissioner Christine Varney views consumer education as being essential to protecting consumer privacy in online environments. The FTC's voluntary principles for online networks will address the following issues:

- Consumer expectations for their personal and transactional information
- Consumer control over personal and transactional information
- Appropriate uses of consumer information, including transactional and personality profile information by online service providers and content providers
- Consumer consent requirements
- Access and correction opportunities for personal information on the nets[8]

One thing is certain—a consistent set of rules will be needed for online networks and service providers, rules that are known to both providers and users. The status of one's personal information in the world of electronic communications must be known to users. For example, can the information be accessed by law enforcement agencies? Evidently, yes: America Online was required to turn over its files when the Virginia police came armed with a search warrant. The police were investigating a murder involving a killer who allegedly met his victim through a Net "chat room," in which people with common interests go to talk via their computers. These chat rooms are not and should not be considered "private." People should know that but often they don't. Unless your communications are encrypted or sent anonymously (see Chapter 10), your electronic conversations and e-mail are not private. Diane Goydan of New Jersey found this out the hard way. Ms. Goydan, a married woman, was apparently sending e-mail of a sexually explicit nature to a man she had met through the Net. Unknown to her, her husband managed to retrieve these e-mail messages. He has since filed for divorce, intending to use her e-mail as evidence to support his claim for custody of their two children.

The Response from Government

In 1993, the United States established the Information Infrastructure Task Force (IITF) to address all aspects of creating a national information infrastructure. In Canada, the Information Highway Advisory Council (IHAC) was created in 1994 to develop a strategy for developing the highway. A key issue studied by both countries was privacy and the protection of personal information traveling the highway. One working group of the U.S. IITF's Information Policy Committee is examining privacy on the highway. Likewise, privacy and network security were jointly identified as one of the four operating principles for Canada's strategy on the highway.

While it is understood that the development of the highway will be a collaborative effort between the public and private sectors, it will be funded largely by the latter. Governments cannot afford the massive investments required, estimated at hundreds of billions of dollars. And because the highway will be built through innovation and human imagination, leaving such a massive creative task to government alone would not be advisable. Yet would business, all on its own, develop a Code of Fair Information Practices for the highway? Can the protection of privacy be left to the whims of the marketplace?

The IITF Working Group on Privacy has adapted the OECD's code to better reflect the realities of electronically networked environments. But even government efforts have been weak. While the goal was laudable, the product was not. The working group's draft Principles for Providing and Using Personal Information was criticized for diluting the time-honored Code of Fair Information Practices, which confers rights on data subjects and responsibilities on data users. The draft was instead directed at data subjects (as well as data users), who were expected to assume greater responsibility for the protection of their personal information. Granted, this may become an unavoidable reality in a highly networked world, where the occurrence of multiple disclosures is the norm, but it sends out a bad message—one that diminishes the amount of responsibility data users should properly assume. From a privacy perspective, shifting responsibility away from the collectors and users of personal information is a poor direction to follow. Consumers can scarcely be held responsible for the fate of their information when it is in the hands of organizations over which they have no control.

The Electronic Privacy Information Center (EPIC), a public interest research group that advances civil liberties in the electronic age, analyzed the working group's draft privacy code and concluded that it fell well short of the mark:

> The principles proposed by the Privacy Working Group are weaker than the current codes, and leave large gaps in National Information Infrastructure (NII) privacy policy in such areas as encryption, informed consent, unique identifiers, and enforcement. The proposed code is also inadequate for the purpose of promoting international data laws, and may limit the ability of users in the United States to exchange data with users in other countries. Unless a stronger code is developed, there will be inadequate privacy protection for future users of the NII.[9]

The code has been revised, and while improvements have been made, it is still viewed as falling short of what is needed. Responsibility for following Fair Information Practices by users of personal information continues to be weak in that shared responsibility with data subjects is still envisioned. Further, the principles do not mandate a right of correction. Individuals would only be granted the opportunity "to correct information that could harm them." However, there is a restriction: the opportunity to correct personal information will depend on "the seriousness of the consequences to the individual of the use of the information." Since it is critical that the volumes of personal information amassed about us be as accurate as possible, this restriction is regrettable.

In the meantime, EPIC has developed its own model privacy code for the information highway, which we would be wise to consider.

EPIC Model Privacy Code for the National Information Infrastructure

1. The confidentiality of electronic communications should be protected.

2. Privacy considerations must be recognized explicitly in the

provision, use, and regulation of telecommunications services.

3. The collection of personal data for telecommunications services should be limited to the extent necessary to provide the service.

4. Service providers should not disclose information without the explicit consent of service users. Service providers should be required to make known their data collection practices to service users.

5. Users should not be required to pay for routine privacy protection. Additional costs for privacy should be imposed only for extraordinary protection.

6. Service providers should be encouraged to explore technical means to protect privacy.

7. Appropriate security policies should be developed to protect network communications.

8. A mechanism should be established to ensure the observance of these principles.

Another group, the National Information Infrastructure Advisory Council (NIIAC), has also produced a set of privacy principles for the highway through one of its subcommittees— Mega Project III. These principles are considered to be superior to the IITF's Privacy Working Group in that they are more encompassing in the range of protections recommended. The principles start by saying that personal privacy "must be protected in the design, management, and use of the [NII]. Informed, uncoerced consent to the use of personally identifiable information, as well as autonomy and individual choice are fostered by ensuring privacy on the NII." These principles also emphasize the importance of privacy to engendering public confidence: "The privacy of communications, information, and transactions must be protected to engender public confidence in the use of the NII. For instance, people should be able to encrypt lawful communications, information, and transactions on the NII." Harry Hammitt, editor of *Access Reports,* feels that implicit in these principles is the view that lack of confidence in the security of sensitive information traveling the highway will be a "make or break" issue for its success. Both individuals and commercial users will be unwilling to use it if security is not strong.

These principles also provide for the right to access your personal information and the right to correct any inaccuracies. In addition, the NIIAC recommends that individuals be informed of other uses of their personal information; secondary uses should not be permitted without informed consent: "Personally identifiable information about an individual provided or generated for one purpose should not be used for an unrelated purpose or disclosed to another party without the informed consent of the individual, except as provided under existing law."

Mega Project III's privacy principles would offer considerable protections on the highway, but more important is whether the Clinton administration will act on any of the principles proposed. Robert Gellman, a Washington-based information and privacy specialist and former chief counsel to the House of Representatives subcommittee on information, justice, and transportation, thinks not. Gellman believes that everyone is simply going through the motions, creating the impression that privacy issues are being taken seriously, when in fact they are not: "So what did the IITF Privacy Working Group propose? Who cares? What we have is a report prepared by bureaucrats who were given no clear direction, no high-level attention, and no political support. It is one of three disjointed privacy efforts under way. No political appointee in the Clinton administration has been willing to devote any time or attention to these principles or to privacy."[10] Let's hope that changes, and changes soon. For as things stand now, Gellman's view is that the privacy principles proposed for the highway are weaker than those required under the existing Privacy Act.

The Intercom Test Drive and Other Trials

A consortium called Intercom Ontario is speeding up the delivery of the information highway to households. The consortium is made up of more than 30 public and private organizations such as telephone companies, software developers, computer companies, real estate developers, retailers, businesses, broadcasters, market researchers, health industry participants, universities, educators, and government.

The consortium plans to run a field trial that will provide "a true test of the city of the future," one of the first simulations of future work and play on the highway. The trial is envisioned for a suburban development made up of "smart" but affordable homes connected to numerous businesses, libraries, schools, universities, museums, galleries, and such. The network will provide learning materials and information, home banking and shopping, personal communications such as e-mail and video-conferencing, and entertainment and leisure pursuits. A "multinet controller" will provide access to four personal networks—TVs, computers, "smart appliances," and wireless communicators—that can be used throughout the home.

Transactions will be carried out through smart cards and other "appliances." Electronic software agents, referred to as "your personal concierge," will store the user's personality profile and permit any other terminal accessed on the trial network, including public ones, to immediately configure themselves to the user's work and play preferences. A great deal of transactional data will be created, stored, and analyzed. Personality profiles? Accessible by all? The consortium's promotional literature states:

> Transactions will be mediated by a "smart" user interface that will dynamically configure itself to the user's work and play patterns; the family member's "appliance" or personal concierge will become simpler to use and more intuitive with each session. A smart card will store the user's personality profile, and allow any other public terminals accessed on the trial network to immediately configure itself to the user's accustomed screens and preferences.[11]

But while the technology is exciting and the opportunities far-reaching, Intercom's literature makes no mention of any measures to safeguard users' privacy or plans to develop Fair Information Practices. What controls will there be to prevent anyone from tapping into the system and accessing people's private information? How will confidentiality be safeguarded? We hope these questions will be addressed up front, at the design stage. Later might be too late.

Several other trials are already taking place. Le Groupe Videotron cable company is making two-way interactive television available to some 34,000 households in Chicoutimi, Quebec. It hopes to expand the delivery of these services, called UBI (universal, bidirectional, interactive), to 1.5 million households throughout Quebec by 2002. The range of services consists of electronic banking and shopping, sending e-mail, regulating home thermostats, accessing stock market reports, skimming through advertising fliers, making printouts of store coupons, and ordering videos through the TV set. ("Video on demand" is already available to cable subscribers in several American cities.)

The one thing that is distinctive about the UBI trial is that its creators devoted considerable thought to the question of privacy and the need to develop a code of conduct. UBI is working with the University of Montreal's Public Law Research Center to develop a code of ethics for the trial. Privacy and data protection were a condition of partnership in the project right from the start.

Smart Cards, Smart Agents, Intelligent Appliances

> With technology transforming our homes into glass houses, what should the rule book say about privacy? With the set-top box digesting huge amounts of information about consumers, the box becomes a camera in the home.[12]

Smart cards are plastic cards, typically the size of a credit card, containing one or more tiny microchips. The microchip is what makes the card "smart," transforming it into a miniature computer that can collect, store, and often process data. Invented more than 20 years ago by Roland Moreno, smart cards are now beginning to gain more popularity in North America, with Visa and MasterCard having recently announced that they will be implementing smart card technology in future cards. Smart cards may be used as either a technology of privacy or a technology of surveillance, depending on whether the information collected is encrypted, whether it resides only on the card itself (privacy-protective), or is transmitted to a central database (facilitating tracking and monitoring of your activities). Take the example of a health smart card that contains your complete medical history. A self-contained record might be very useful to have on you in an emergency, but would you want all the details of your medical records transmitted to some central location, accessible by network, where countless others unknown to you could have access to that information?

Along with the information highway and networked communications comes a new device, known variously as a smart agent, interface agent, agent-based interface, intelligent interface, information appliance, or digital butler, to help you sift through the barrage of information that will descend upon you and leave you with only what you truly want.

Your smart agent will indeed be "smart" in that it will learn about you over time and adapt its programmed profile of you as the "relationship" develops. Your agent will probably become an indispensable tool for navigating your way through the staggering amounts of unwanted noise on the highway.

Nicholas Negroponte predicts that smart agents will become indispensable tools in a fully networked world, to manage the constant assault of incoming information. He views them as being "the unequivocal future of computing." These agents would function much like filters—keeping out what you don't want, but also making sure that you get what you *do* want. Your agent would navigate its way through the sea of information out there, identify what you're interested in, and then prioritize it for your reading and viewing pleasure. Your own personal editor, Negroponte predicts, will then watch television for you, read newspapers for you, and create your personalized viewing program and news summary. "Digital butlers will be numerous, living both in the network and by your side....Imagine a future in which your interface agent can read every newswire and newspaper and catch every TV and radio broadcast on the planet, and then construct a personalized summary."[13]

Negroponte envisions two types of agents: one that stays at home by your side (on your wrist or in your pocket) and one that lives on the Net, surfing on your behalf. While the homebody agent could be "hermetically sealed," posing few threats to your privacy, the messenger agent is another matter, since it would be accessible to others traveling the Net, as would all the information it holds about you. Negroponte says these "net-dwelling" agents are the ones we need to worry about.

To be truly useful in its role, your personal agent has to learn all about you. But how do you keep all that information truly tamper-proof? Negroponte predicts "a whole new business in confiding our profiles to a trusted third party, which will behave like a Swiss bank."[14] But right now there are few credible, trustworthy third parties who can be entrusted with your secrets. Another model that is unfolding is not to entrust your private information to anyone, but rather to protect it through encryption (discussed in Chapter 10).

Smart agents may become much needed and much welcomed on the highway, but we cannot emphasize enough the inherent privacy nightmare if the information known to our agents ended up in the wrong hands. At a 1995 conference on privacy and security, Whitfield Diffie, the inventor of public key encryption, questioned whether smart agents would be working for us or for some other third party. Diffie says that the types of devices to appear in the near future in the form of set-top boxes on our TVs will be working not for us but for the cable companies—a potential window into our homes and into our lives. In *The Virtual Community*, Howard Rheingold argues that although this technology isn't an essential ingredient for surveillance to take place, "it sure makes surveillance easier when you invite the surveillance device into your home."[15]

Right now, most of your information and personal communications are not encrypted. And in order to weed out what you don't want, your agent will have to "know" exactly what you do want; it will have to know intimately what you are interested in. Will anyone else have access to this intimate knowledge about you? If so, will you get to decide who? Many companies would like to know about your consumer habits.

The chairman of the Home Shopping Network, Barry Diller, says that his company would like to build detailed profiles of its customers, which customers could use for a wide range of services. But the Home Shopping Network undoubtedly wants to use this information too. When asked about the privacy implications of these profiles, a spokesman for the network acknowledged that the security of the data would be paramount: "We are very aware of the trust issue and we consider it one of the more important issues in the system design. Customers would have to have utter and total confidence that the information they provide is secure."[16]

How to build this confidence will become a key focus for business, since consumers are very concerned about the dwindling prospects for their privacy on the highway. (Chapter 7 discusses consumer privacy in greater depth.) In 1994, a public opinion poll on the information highway conducted by Andersen Consulting found an unprecedented level of concern about privacy: 85 percent of those surveyed reported that they were worried about their privacy on the highway. This finding surprised even those who had commissioned the survey. (The newspaper headline aptly read "Snoopophobia Haunts Information Highway: 85% fear new network will mean loss of privacy.")

Privacy on the Highway: Will There Be Any?

Privacy as we know it may not exist in the next decade if we don't take some action now to ensure it is protected. Will the new technologies serve our needs or dictate them? Will we all fall onto the path of technological determinism that seems to have cast its spell on so many—seeking a technological fix for all that ails us? One policy paper on the information highway paints a rather grim picture:

> While each technology brings different capabilities, they all contribute to a completely unprecedented capacity for the surveillance of every man, woman, and child, whether as customer, student, employee, patient, taxpayer, or recipient

of government services....It is this growing trend for information systems to place limits on our freedom, on our life's potential, that privacy advocates and science fiction writers alike find utterly chilling.[17]

You may still find it hard to fathom how so much information about your habits and preferences could be learned in the ways that we've described. Maybe it sounds like paranoia to you. Perhaps a few scenarios might help convince you. The first one is hypothetical but very close to being real.

Francesca, who normally buys her lingerie from the Victoria's Secret mail-order catalog, can now place her orders through her TV set-top box. What's more, she can view the items in motion—far better than browsing through pictures in the catalog. So Francesca gets out her credit card, punches the numbers into the keyboard, and orders a number of items. Later that evening, she orders several erotic movies from the hundreds of video selections now directly available to her. No need to go down to the video store and feel uncomfortable at the counter. She can now push a button for everything from her home—no one need know of her affinity for lace, or her viewing preferences, or her choice of erotic reading material (which she ordered through her set-top box last week). And all this from the privacy of her own home. Well, not exactly.

It may be true that Francesca need not face anyone when placing these orders, but that's about the extent of the privacy she will enjoy. She would have had much more privacy if she had bought her purchases in person, and paid cash for them. What she doesn't know (and hasn't asked) is what will happen to the information about her orders—what's known as her transaction-generated information. These transactions reflect her personal preferences and point to a certain lifestyle, real or imagined. She may think that once she places her order and pays for her merchandise, that's the end of it. But she's wrong—that's just the beginning.

Direct marketers on the highway may be interested in knowing about Francesca's habits. So might her employer (a school board) and her insurance company (aware of health risks associated with a promiscuous lifestyle). But who said she was promiscuous? A data profile, of course, is never an exact replica of the real thing; assumptions have to be made and inferences drawn on the basis of point-of-sale transactions and previous patterns.

The following not-so-hypothetical scenario is based on a little-known form of surveillance used by law enforcement agencies called Realtime Residential Power Line Surveillance (RRPLS). New smart meters are enhancing the ability to collect data that indicate what electrical appliances a resident of a particular home uses and at what time of day. When combined with other transactional data, RRPLS becomes a powerful window into your activities. Consider the following example from Rick Crawford:

> Contrary to a household's normal pattern, one of its occupants, a 43-year-old married male (according to his driver's license data) arises early one Saturday morning, showers, shaves with his electric razor, and irons some clothes. He buys gas in town, then that night pays for two dinners and two tickets to a show (all on his credit card). After returning home, the stereo is turned on (a rare event according to his RRPLS file). The data from the waterbed indicates an unusual night—every time the sheets are thrown back, the RRPLS detects the waterbed heater cycling. The next morning, data indicates an unusually long shower, followed by two uses of the hair dryer. The second use is much longer than normal for the male occupant, indicating he probably shared the shower with a long-haired person.

> During this time, commercial transaction records indicate the occupant's wife is halfway around the globe, on a business trip paid for by her employer. RRPLS data from her hotel room also indicate an overnight visitor. Within days, the couple is inundated with direct-mail solicitation from divorce lawyers.[18]

Have you taken a long shower lately?...Longer than usual?

Lastly, we offer three seemingly far-fetched developments. But the implications are far-reaching. In the June 1994 issue of *Privacy Journal*, editor Robert Ellis Smith reported on a new microchip that could be inserted into breast implants. The chip contains a 10-digit serial number, presumably to permit tracking the implants in the event of a recall. But surely there are other ways of determining what kind of implant a person has—such as looking in one's medical file, or just asking the patient. Do we really want parts of our bodies to be as "readable" as the bar codes on supermarket products? "A low-frequency hand-held scanner can read an individual's code when it is passed over the microchip beneath the skin—much like a supermarket bar-code reader."[19]

Such a microchip may strike you as some type of gimmick, but two doctors in the United States recently had a microchip containing their respective medical histories implanted in their bodies, as part of a trial. House pets in Europe and North America are routinely implanted with microchips that identify their owners. When a group of internationally renowned privacy experts met to discuss the privacy implications of the information highway, they expressed concern that "these tracking systems will be adapted to humans. The conversion would not be difficult." Among the many who shared this view was Simon Davies, the director general of Privacy International, who was dismayed that a number of professionals he had spoken to would not object to such a tracking system. In an increasingly networked world, information resulting from such tracking systems could easily be communicated to anyone, anywhere, creating a scenario for total surveillance.

Another technological development, the *transponder*, is a communications device which allows stationary and moving objects to be located by sending a signal to a remote location. When attached to objects, animals, or people, it helps locate them. Transponders are being implanted at a growing rate into the bodies of pets and livestock to locate and identify them if they are lost. One company, Newchild International, has developed a transponder device called Park Pal to help locate children or the elderly "who might wander away while on a family outing." At first, Newchild had considered marketing this product only to the tourism and theme park industry. However, the technology has attracted interest from the military, communications, security, and entertainment sectors. Just think of the applications!

Today, it may seem far-fetched, but how long before the microchip embedded in the breast implant and the transponder carried by children are merged into one unit? How long before one device can be implanted into our bodies to identify and track us, and to transmit this information electronically to a central database?

Concluding Thought

If you're going to shop, bank, date, or communicate on the highway, do so with your eyes wide open. Do you want to leave a digital data trail behind you? Do you want everyone to have access to your transactional data? Put on your virtual seat belt. The information highway promises to transform your everyday television set into two-way interactive media. Watching TV will never be the same again...nor will your private life.

Endnotes

1. Thomas B. Riley, "Information Technology and Privacy Protection," paper presented at the Privacy and Technology Conference, Ottawa, September 30, 1994, p. 2.
2. Nicholas Negroponte, *Being Digital* (New York: Knopf, 1995).
3. Paul Hoffert, quoted in Andrew Coyne, "The Information Highwayman Comes Riding," *Globe and Mail*, October 1, 1994.
4. Evan Hendricks, "On-Line: Microsoft Won't Sell Customer Names," *Privacy Times*, August 2, 1995, p. 2.
5. Hendricks, "On-Line," p. 3.
6. Ibid.
7. Bill Gates, "Privacy: Who Should Know What About Whom," *New York Times*, September 15, 1995.
8. "Federal Trade Commission's New Initiative Solidifies Its Privacy Leadership Role," *Privacy and American Business*, Vol. 2, No. 3 (October 1995), p. 3.

9. Electronic Privacy Information Center, "Privacy Guidelines for the National Information Infrastructure: A Review of the Proposed Principles of the Privacy Working Group," Report 94-1, (unpublished, 1994), p. 1.

10. Robert M. Gellman, "Prescribing Privacy: The Uncertain Role of the Physician in the Protection of Patient Privacy," *North Carolina Law Review*, 62 (1984):255, 274–278.

11. Intercom Ontario Project, "City of the Future Tested by Groundbreaking Canadian Consortium" (April 1994).

12. Ken Auletta, "Under the Wire: Will the Telecommunications Revolution End in Monopoly or Big Brotherhood?" *The New Yorker*, January 17, 1994, p. 53.

13. Nicholas Negroponte, "Prime Time Is My Time," *Wired* (August 1994), p. 134.

14. Nicholas Negroponte, "Less Is More: Interfact Agents as Digital Butlers," *Wired* (June 1994), p. 142.

15. Howard Rheingold, *The Virtual Community: Homesteading on the Electronic Frontier* (Reading, Mass.: Addison Wesley, 1993).

16. Evan Hendricks, "QVC: Your Profile," *Privacy Times*, October 21, 1994.

17. Industry Canada, "Privacy and the Canadian Information Highway: Building Canada's Information and Communications Infrastructure" (October 1994).

18. Rick Crawford, "Techno Prisoners," *Adbusters Quarterly* (Summer 1994), pp. 21–22.

19. Robert Ellis Smith, "Implanting ID Microchips in Humans No Longer Far-Fetched," *Privacy Journal*, Vol. 20, No. 8 (June 1994).

Consumer Privacy:
What You Should Know

The consumer pays for every purchase twice over: first with
money, and second, with information that's worth money.
ALVIN TOFFLER

Privacy has already been penetrated in more subtle, complex ways.
This assault on privacy, invisible to most, takes place in the broad
daylight of everyday life. The weapons are cash registers and credit
cards. When Big Brother arrives, don't be surprised if he looks like
a grocery clerk, because privacy has been turning into a commodi-
ty, courtesy of better and better information networks, for years.
HOWARD RHEINGOLD

Privacy has been described as the consumer issue of the 1990s.
Our concern is somewhat ironic, because we are often responsible for the intrusions into our privacy in the marketplace—
through our everyday transactions. Most of us accept that a certain amount of information must be relinquished in exchange
for desired goods and services. Some information is, understandably, necessary for transactions to be carried out. If you
want to buy something with your credit card, your card number
must be recorded by the store so it can collect payment. But
should the company also use the record of your transactions to
create a personal profile of your buying habits?

Two of the key Fair Information Practices are: collect only
the information that is truly needed, and use that information
only for the purpose for which it was collected. Thus, in the
case of a purchase made with a credit card, any use of your
information without your consent beyond the purpose of col-

lecting payment is a secondary use, not in accordance with Fair Information Practices. Your consent, however, is rarely sought for such routine occurrences as creating customer profiles or compiling names and addresses into mailing lists. Your information is regularly sold or rented to other companies for their commercial gain.

With fewer people protected by the anonymity of using cash for their purchases, concern for privacy arises each time you use your credit or debit card. Electronic forms of payment identify you and leave a data trail. With the escalating capacity of information technologies to record and analyze transactional data, link databases, create personal profiles, and predict your behavior on the basis of past purchases and transactions, the trail of digital information you leave behind you compounds the problem of privacy. As we move closer and closer to a cashless society, eventually all our shopping will be monitored.

What the Polls Say: People Are Worried

Lest there be any doubt as to the growing concern over privacy, let us put it to rest. Recent consumer polls and surveys in both the United States and in Canada show a steady increase in concern for privacy. Robert Gellman, former chief counsel to a congressional subcommittee, noted, "Public opinion polls have shown a tremendous rise in the general level of concern about the loss of privacy, starting in the late 1970s and continuing in the 1990s."

In the United States, surveys conducted by Louis Harris and Associates have shown a progressive increase in the public's concern for privacy, up from 67 percent in 1978 to 84 percent in 1994. A review of this trend noted that "people seem to believe that the loss of privacy will become an even greater problem in the future than it was in the 1980s."[1]

A 1992 survey by Louis Harris and Equifax, a leading consumer credit information service, found that the American public's concern with threats to their privacy remained consistently high—78 percent in 1992 versus 79 percent in 1991 and 1990. Much of the concern revolved around the security of personal information in computers, with 89 percent believing that computers had made it easier for someone to improperly access confidential information. Seventy-six percent of respondents felt that consumers had lost all control of the way their personal information was being used and exchanged by companies. The 1995 Equifax-Harris Mid-Decade Consumer Privacy Survey found consistently high levels of concern for privacy (82 percent), with 80 percent of Americans believing they had lost all control over their personal information.

Another 1995 privacy survey by Yankelovich Partners, found that 90 percent of Americans were in favor of legislation to protect them from businesses invading their privacy. This finding was surprisingly similar to an earlier survey conducted by Time/CNN in 1991, which found that "Americans' concerns for their privacy was rising and they wanted strict controls over others' use of their personal information."[2] In response to the question "Should companies that sell information to others be required by law to ask permission from individuals before making the information available?" a resounding 93 percent said yes. Further, 88 percent felt that companies that intended to sell their information should be legislated to make that information available to data subjects so they would have the opportunity to correct any errors.

In 1993, Ekos Research released its report *Privacy Revealed*, which showed consumer concern for privacy to be very high: 92 percent expressed concern about their personal privacy (52 percent reporting "extreme concern"); 81 percent felt they should be informed in advance when their personal information was being collected; 83 percent felt strongly that their permission should be obtained before an organization shared their information with others; and 87 percent strongly believed that they should be told how information obtained from them would be used.

Control—having it and preserving it—figured highly in all these findings. Among the factors identified as capable of diminishing people's levels of concern was control: "Consent, control, and regulation: privacy intrusions, particularly those involving personal information, are much more acceptable when people have some sense of control over the process. This sense of control can be drawn from the right to consent, or from some form of regulation."[3]

Database Marketing, Direct Marketing, Telemarketing

"Does it seem as if a lot of companies are taking quite a friendly interest in your life these days?" a *Business Week* cover story asks. Database marketing is nothing new, except that today much more refined techniques are being used to identify expressly targeted sectors and individuals. This precisely directed intrusion into our lives has been called many things: niche marketing, one-to-one marketing, relationship marketing, dialogue marketing, and loyalty marketing (accompanied, not surprisingly, by loyalty engineering departments).

Much faster computers, combined with parallel computing and new information techniques, enable marketers to identify smaller and smaller "niches" of the population, ultimately zeroing in or "drilling down" to the individual level. The ability for "data mining" represents considerable progress from mass marketing (where undifferentiated consumers all receive identical solicitations) and market segmentation (consumers being broken down into smaller segments based on common demographic features—they live in the same neighborhood; they all bought Toyotas). Companies say that now they can get to know you much better and develop a relationship with you, just like in the good old days of the corner grocer. But the corner grocer had limited knowledge about you, information that you would have chosen to impart to him. You also would have known something about him.

Privacy Alert: A Consumer's Guide to Privacy in the Marketplace, an innovative report by the Information and Privacy Commission of Ontario, starts out by asking, "How did they get my name? This is the consumer chant of the '90s, and it is quickly evolving into 'Who doesn't have my name?'

Few have escaped it because these days, your name is worth its weight in gold." This isn't far from the truth: in the United States, the direct-marketing industry is estimated to generate annual sales in excess of $75 billion. Direct marketing has become an extremely competitive and aggressive business, and people's privacy is more an annoyance than a concern to most companies.

The direct-marketing sector isn't covered by any privacy laws. Although several bills have been introduced in the United States to strengthen consumers' rights to privacy, they have always been defeated. Representative Dean Gallo, who introduced such a bill in 1994 in response to constituents' complaints about junk mail, captured the essence of the problem when he said, "Consumers have a right to know that when they sign a guest book at a hotel, or apply for a credit card, or order from a catalog, that the information they provide is going to be compiled and sold to any company that has a few dollars to pay for it."

Both the U.S. Direct Marketing Association (DMA) and the Canadian Direct Marketing Association (CDMA) have tried to address the increase in consumer concern by developing their own privacy codes. In addition, both the DMA and the CDMA offer a Do Not Mail/Do Not Call service which allows consumers to indicate that they do not wish to be solicited. These are both positive and commendable measures, but are they enough? As marketing tactics become more sophisticated, and privacy more difficult to protect, marketers will try to ensure that staying anonymous doesn't get any easier.

Opting In Versus Opting Out: What's the Difference?

One solution to prevent your information from being misused is for companies to seek your consent to use it for additional (secondary) purposes such as direct-marketing solicitations. This can be done in two ways.

Opting in requires you to let the company know that you consent to the subsequent use of your information; that is, you have to say "count me in" if you wish to receive marketing information from other companies (positive consent). Without such a positive indication, the organization assumes that you do not wish to have your information given to other companies for other purposes. This is the system used by the German postal services. If you have not provided them with prior written consent, your name and address will not be passed on to third parties.

In short, you get to choose, to decide what you want done with your information. As Professor Oscar Gandy notes in his comprehensive analysis of the uses and abuses of personal information, *The Panoptic Sort*, "It is not unreasonable to assume that individuals would be the best judge of when they are the most interested and therefore the most receptive to information of a particular kind. Others with information to provide ought to assume that, unless requested, no information is desired. This would be the positive option....Individuals should be free to choose when they are ready to enter the market for information."[4]

The second method, *opting out*, also permits you to make a choice, but there is a subtle difference. Here you have to inform an organization of your wish *not* to have your information passed on to others, usually by checking off a box. If you don't check off the box—if you don't say "count me out"—the organization is free to use your information in any way it wishes. Beware, though: an opt-out box isn't always on the form, and sometimes even if it is, it's buried in the small print.

Thus, the difference between opting in and opting out is the type of action that needs to be taken to convey your wishes. The importance of one over the other hinges on the default that kicks in, which is the basic difference between the two. But oh, what a difference!

From a privacy perspective, the ideal choice is the positive consent, "count me in" option. You can't opt in by accident; you have to specifically request solicitations to receive them. Marketers, however, dread the thought of positive consent becoming a widely accepted standard, fearing that it will put them out of business, even though the goal of marketers to reach only those who are likely to be interested in their solicitations seems quite compatible with this option. It stands to reason that if you want to hear more about a product or service that interests you, you will ask to receive information about it. Using ourselves as examples, we *want* to be put on mailing lists for future privacy conferences, workshops on networked communications, and publications on these subjects. But that may not apply to you. Instead, you might want to be informed of all special offers to locations where you enjoy vacationing, or advance opportunities to buy theater tickets.

Marketers argue that any intrusions arising from the sale of mailing lists are justified by the benefit to consumers in the form of special offers and special products. There may well be potential gains for those interested in receiving such offers, but these gains would also be obtained from offering consumers the choice of positive consent. Legal scholar Anne Wells Branscomb argues that the information industry would be well served if it started to treat consumers as equal partners:

> The information industry must not become a Peeping Tom whom we must catch in the act of violating our privacy. It must seek to become a responsible partner, helping us find the information that will allow us to make reasonable purchases of things we need or want at prices we can afford. American consumers are avid shoppers, more likely to opt into than out of the information marketplace.[5]

The bottom line is, if you want something, you'll do something to get it. If you're not interested, then perhaps marketers are wasting their resources trying to reel you in. And at times, they may inadvertently cause great heartache through their efforts.

Marketers can easily obtain lists of expectant mothers, estimate their due dates, and then track children's birthdays. One couple had been successful in keeping their address a secret for security reasons (the husband was a police officer). Within 6 weeks of having a baby, the woman was inundated with junk mail aimed at new mothers. It turns out that the hospital had sold her name and address to a direct-marketing company, and soon she was added to dozens of mailing lists.

It is not uncommon for direct marketers to send a 1-year birthday card, perhaps accompanied by a promotional offer. Imagine the trauma, however, if the mother had lost her child during pregnancy or at childbirth. The birthday card would automatically roll out in a year's time, causing a tragic reminder of what could have been. Oscar Gandy provides another example that, while far less painful, nonetheless illustrates the vulnerability of certain individuals to common marketing techniques:

> Information about past purchases of chocolate, combined with information that the person is a repeat buyer of "clothing for the big woman," might provide the marketers of chocolate (or other vendors of sweets) with a basis for betting that there may be an interest in their product. Information that indicates this person has also been a customer of several diet and exercise programs and has enrolled in these programs in the late spring of most years may also suggest that her power to resist an appeal is not great....All this information suggests vulnerability. But if this woman is trying to get through this particular winter with her weight under control, she is not likely to seek out this information on her own. With unhindered telemarketing...the positive option is not hers to choose.[6]

Some businesses are beginning to show support for the opt-in model. In addition to Bill Gates' policy for Microsoft Network (see Chapter 6), *USA Today* has favored the opt-in approach for the use of its customers' personal information. The paper said that customers' permission should be obtained prior to renting or selling their personal data for marketing purposes. While this may cause some minor inconvenience for businesses, they asked who should bear the burden: "the businesses that glean the profit, or the consumers whose information is sold?...Opt-in does not trample on anyone's rights. Consumers can still get their catalogs and other direct-mail pitches by checking a box or clicking a mouse. Companies can still get data for marketing by asking for it.... If a business wants the privilege of marketing your most private matters, it should be willing to spend the time it takes to convince you that you'll benefit."[7] Progressive businesses such as these see the benefits of giving their customers a positive choice, up front, regarding the uses of their personal information.

While most companies have yet to offer us the opt-in model, there are things you can do right now to protect your information. Scour any form—product warranty card, enrollment form, anything you fill out—for a check-off box that will allow you to opt out. When you find it, check it (that is, if you don't want to receive solicitations). If there is no box, just add one. Simply write on the form that you do not want your personal information used for any other purpose including selling, leasing, or renting it to third parties. It might help to draw further attention to this by highlighting it with a bright marker or writing it in red. Your statement will send a clear message to the companies you do business with, and if they value your business, they will listen.

Already, more and more businesses are becoming aware of the need to tell you that they won't be passing on your information; a sense of obligation to disclose any secondary uses of your information appears to be growing. In time, standard opt-out clauses may be developed to appear on all forms seeking your personal information. And with the endorsement of a respected body such as the Canadian Standards Association (or perhaps the American National Bureau of Standards), you could take comfort in knowing that any form containing an approved opt-out box would provide you with the protection you needed; you could rely on the fact that information placed on such forms would not result in unwanted solicitations.

The Dollar Value of Your Information

In a factor analysis of responses...to questions about the technology of surveillance, the strongest factor identified was one termed My Business. The factor reflected a general feeling that what people read, the films they viewed, the numbers they called for information, and more generally, how they spent their money were their business, and no one else's.[8]

It's your information...your business. The message is clear. So with that in mind, we want you to think about something. People often ask why businesses should be able to use, sell, and make money from your personal information when you obtain no benefit or compensation for it. The privacy commissioner of Canada has said, "Personal information is the property of the individual to whom it relates." So it only makes sense that you should benefit from the commercial use of your information, information that fuels a multibillion-dollar direct-marketing industry. As Anne Wells Branscomb states in *Who Owns Information?*: "Our names and addresses and personal transactions are valuable information assets worthy of recognition that we have property rights in them. Unless we assert these rights, we will lose them. If such information has economic value, we should receive something of value in return for its use by others."[9] But this is not the case now. Your information is used by others to gain entry into your lives, usually without having been invited.

Think about how this principle applies to your other "possessions." If someone takes a picture of you and wants to reproduce it in a book, he or she would first consult with you and obtain your consent, and you might then be in a position to collect royalties from its use. And there isn't much difference between your pictorial image and your data profile; both are representations of your self. In the U.S. case of *Shilbey v. Time,* "the petitioner claimed that the sale of subscription lists constituted an invasion of privacy because the information about the plaintiff's personality that might be inferred from such a list was the equivalent of an image or likeness, not unlike that provided by a photograph or an artist's rendering."[10]

While the commercial display of a person's photograph may be illegal (without consent), using a person's name or personal preferences for commercial gain without consent is not; this forms the basis of direct-marketing and telemarketing solicitations. But that would all change if it was up to Ram Avrahami, and it may be. Avrahami is in the process of suing *U.S. News & World Report* for selling his name and address to another magazine. Avrahami is charging that the sale of his name violates a Virginia law which requires an individual's express written consent before using his or her name for commercial purposes. The legal challenge of the magazine's sale of customer names and addresses was to be mounted in Arlington County General District Court, but it was later bumped up to the higher U.S. Circuit Court.

Ram Avrahami argues that the sale of his name, without his permission, violates his property rights: "Mr. Avrahami believes he owns his own name—and he contends that if companies want to sell it, he should have the right to either prevent the sale or to be compensated for it."[11] A court date was scheduled for November 27, 1995, but the court granted the magazine's motion for a continuance. The trial was then rescheduled for February 1996, but the district court judge ruled that the lower court did not have jurisdiction to hear this case. It was then scheduled to be heard by the U.S. Circuit Court on June 6, 1996. A favorable outcome in this case could have enormous implications for the future of the direct-marketing industry. Another case recently heard in a California small claims court already has.

Robert Beken of San Diego took Computer City to small claims court for sending him unwanted mail solicitations, and he won. On January 3, 1996, Judge Jerome Varon ordered Computer City to pay Beken $1000 in damages plus court costs. Here's what happened. In April 1995, Beken bought something at Computer City and paid for it by check. When he gave the check to the clerk, he noticed the clerk keying in his name and address into the computer. Beken asked if he was being added to a mailing list, to which the clerk answered no. At this point Beken quickly took back his check and wrote the following on the back: "Computer City agrees *not* to place Robert Beken on any mailing list or send him any advertisements or mailings. Computer City agrees that a breach of this agreement by Computer City will damage Robert Beken and that these damages may be pursued in court. Further, that these damages for the first breach are $1000. The deposit of this check for payment is agreement with these terms and conditions." The clerk discussed this with a fellow employee but accepted the check without dispute.

In the following months Beken received four mail solicitations from Computer City. Beken sent two letters of protest, both of which remained unanswered. By November, he'd had enough; Beken took his case to court. The presiding judge agreed with him. Judge Varon was satisfied that what Beken had written on the back of the check had created a contract, which store personnel had accepted. The judge ruled that Computer City breached that contract by placing Beken on a mailing list and sending him unwanted mail. Beken was awarded $1000 in damages plus court costs.

This case represents a victory for consumers tired of receiving mounds of junk mail. Comments in favor of this case have ranged from *USA Today*: "For anyone tired of emptying wastebaskets laden with unwanted mail, the efforts of Beken, Avrahami, and others deserve a cheer," to Beth Givens, the director of the California Privacy Rights Clearinghouse: "Is this a significant victory? I think so. A court has agreed that a consumer has a right to say 'no' to junk mail and to have the request honored. Perhaps this case, along with the Avrahami case, will serve as wake-up calls to the direct-marketing industry. Consumers want and deserve to be able to control what enters their mailboxes." Of that there is no doubt.

As things stand now, however, not only are you rarely given any financial remuneration for the commercial uses of your information, but it is used as the vehicle by which to bombard you with such annoyances as junk mail and telemarketers calling at all hours. These daily intrusions into your lives are not only a nuisance but to some an outrage, because your personal information is being used as the point of entry—as the vehicle with which to peer into your lives.

But if you *want* to let them in, then a case can be made that (1) the choice to have your information used for secondary purposes should be yours to make—you should be able to veto some uses up front, and (2) if you consent to further uses, then *you* should obtain some financial remuneration for the commercial uses of your information, perhaps in the form of modest royalties.

Collecting Royalties for Your Information

A royalty system has been proposed for the commercial uses of your personal information (your property) by sociologists Ken Laudon, Gary Marx, and James Rule. Lawrence Hunter and James Rule suggest that what is needed is a property right for personal information, similar to the property rights we already enjoy and over which we have some control.[12] Under this right, every person would own the rights to commercial exploitation of her or his personal information, and these rights could be retained or sold, much like mineral rights or movie rights.

Yet privacy, when treated as a fundamental human right, should not be traded away to the highest bidder; it is not a commodity. Especially in the context of the rights of citizens in relation to the state, privacy should not even be put on the table for negotiation. This would threaten any legislated protections already in place. As Professor Eli Noam, an expert on telecommunications privacy, noted: "A distribution of privacy rights on a free-market basis would provide no protection for citizens against encroachment by the state. The only effective limits on government are those established through constitutional means. Therefore, any system which allocates privacy according to the open market would also need constitutional provisions barring infringements by the state."[13] Any consideration of economic gain in exchange for our personal information should be made only in the private sector, in the context of commercial transactions. Legislated protections must continue to safeguard our fundamental rights, and restrictions on the uses of our information must continue to apply to government organizations.

But with respect to the *commercial* uses of our personal information, a property right to personal information, which in turn would ensconce the right to control our property, might be a good idea. In an interview with Don Tapscott on September

25, 1995, Esther Dyson, chair of the Electronic Frontier
Foundation and president of EDventure Holdings Inc. promot-
ed the notion of information as property: "I'd rather have a
much simpler piece of legislation that says information about a
person is that person's property and then each individual could
control how his information is going to be treated."

This notion of information as property (or what some call
transaction-generated privacy) has been criticized because it
would burden the poor disproportionately. While there may be
some truth to this, who should be making these decisions? As
Eli Noam astutely points out, "A poor person's priorities may
often not include privacy protection....The poor are best
helped by more money; to micromanage their condition
through restricting their right to transact may well end up a
patronizing social policy and inefficient economic policy."[14]

In any event, the present-day reality is one in which the
personal information of the public—both rich and poor—is
being freely used, without any financial gain to the individuals
involved. Clearly, all consumers would benefit from a royalty
system for the commercial uses of their personal information.

Hunter and Rule's proposed royalty scheme parallels the
system of paying royalties to musicians each time their songs
are played on the radio. You the consumer would first be given
the choice of whether you wished to have your information
used for a secondary purpose. If you agreed to the particular
use, then you would be told what amount of compensation or
royalty you could expect to receive. You could then decide if you
wanted to proceed. If you consented, each use of your personal
information would be monitored, and modest payments made.

Alternatively, Dyson suggests that the big credit bureaus and
information services such as Equifax and TRW could shift their
focus—working for the individuals whose information they collect, and representing them in the sale and management of
their information, much like information brokers. Just as banks
get paid for managing your money, information brokers could
get a small percentage for managing your information and selling it, for example, to a mail-order catalog house. "It would add
a little money to my account and add a commission to its own

account," Dyson notes. But the beauty of such a model is that your information would be managed according to *your* instructions: you would decide *if* and to whom you wanted the information sold. Control over your personal information would reside with you, the true owner of the information.

Establishing such a property right would also give you grounds to insist on knowing how your information was obtained (as in, "How did they get my name?") when approached with a solicitation based on access to your personal information. Such a question is a perfectly legitimate one to ask, and the likelihood of getting an accurate answer under such a scheme as proposed above is far greater than at the present time.

Such schemes would be no more complicated to organize than the highly complex, sophisticated systems now used for database marketing and exchange. In 1991, the U.S. Congressional Research Service recognized the technical feasibility of considering individuals' proprietary interest in their personal data. It said that modern data processing technology that commercially trades personal data in increasingly complex, rapid, and efficient ways could easily be modified to include "provisions to account for the proprietary interest of the individuals whom the data describe. Such provisions could be seen as adjusting the balance between personal proprietary interests and the interests of commercial compilers and marketers of personal data."[15]

Professor Ken Laudon also argues in favor of treating personal information as a form of property, and proposes market-based mechanisms for compensating individuals for their information.

In fact, the first royalty payment system has already appeared. A company in Cambridge, Massachusetts, offers an online service that provides precise data about consumers' choices and pays royalties to consumers for the commercial use of their information. Although this system differs somewhat from the model proposed by Hunter and Rule, it is nonetheless one in which the personal preferences that consumers display toward a particular product or service (and which are captured in an "interaction behavior" profile) actually bring in some cash. This is one of the first systems in which individuals are given some form of monetary remuneration for indicating their likes and dislikes, and having them sold to commercial vendors. It's a step in the right direction, according to one individual who wrote to *Privacy Journal*. He wanted to know when commercial enterprises would realize that there was always a cost associated with the raw materials of doing business, including information. "Either the commercial interests involved will quit using my personal information without my expressed consent, or else they will compensate me in a direct monetary manner for the use of the information. (One of these days I'm going to copyright my personal information and give it legal standing.)"[16]

The Internet: A Marketer's Dream… A Consumer's Nightmare?

If the person quoted above thinks that his personal information shouldn't be used by businesses without his consent or some monetary compensation, then he should stay away from the Internet. The ability to track consumers' personal preferences, likes, and dislikes has never been greater. Net services—which, for example, track the "clickstream" of traffic to some 14,000 Usenet news groups—are beginning to proliferate. Software tools such as Webtrac and Netcount track the items you click on when browsing the World Wide Web. "Dejanews" is a service which makes a copy of all postings to Usenet news groups and then makes this information available on its Web site (http://dejanews.com), along with an index to assist in searches. Not only can searches be done by the names of those who have posted messages, but profiles of users can also be developed. While one may argue that anyone who posts a message to a news group should realize that it cannot be considered to be "private," this may not be evident to all users, especially the uninitiated. A new visitor, for example, to the news group "alt.sex.shy and inhibited" may not realize that sending a message will identify her as a participant. Being a neophyte, she may not be aware of what may be obvious to others. Should she lose all her privacy in the process? Maybe a flashing warning notice should appear on the screen the first time she sends a message, making it perfectly clear what the consequences of such an action will be. User beware.

Regardless of all the hype associated with the information highway, one thing is clear: the Internet will function as its "main artery," certainly in the foreseeable future. What will this mean to consumers keenly awaiting the 500-channel universe and eager to shop through the set-top boxes on their TVs? The October 31, 1995 show of the highly acclaimed public affairs series *Frontline* was devoted to the subject "High Stakes in Cyberspace." It revealed that while individuals exposed to the possibilities of this new technology in their homes were pleased to have many of the conveniences offered, they hadn't given much thought to the potential loss of privacy or its future implications. Nor did they want to become the pawns of advertisers who could prey on their weaknesses by bringing "impulse shopping" right into their homes.

Marketers were quoted as saying, "The people providing the information [the advertisers] can now watch you [the consumer] as *you* watch the information [the ad]." Online services "can know all about you"—as users interact with an ad, responding to questions and providing information, marketers can become familiar with what products they like and dislike, how many children they have, their ages, their home, their pets, how long they lingered on certain products, and more. Some say that the most important services sold by popular search engines such as Yahoo and Lycos will be advertising and data collection—"meta-info," or information about information.

Advertising programs that track the number of "hits" on a client's product and analyze the detailed information provided by consumers can be viewed as a marketer's goldmine. In the words of one marketer, "Rather than have to go out and get the consumers each time, you can train them to come to you." This may be an appealing advantage of online services to marketers, but what about to consumers? Is the vision of the consumer as trained seal an appealing prospect? This is a further example of erosion of control, control that should lie in *your* hands, not the marketers'.

Once they know who and where you are, marketers can then "reverse direct mail" to you, pitching you with products targeted to your specific interests. Later, this information can also be used offline to contact people by phone—"we actually call up our customers." With their consent? Unlikely.

Bell Atlantic is offering its customers a new interactive video service through their televisions called Stargazer which will "bring the video store right into your living room." You will be able to select all your favorites at the push of a button and will be billed only for what you watch (once you've had the TV set-top box installed). The interesting marketing twist is that soon, different types of watching will be offered to viewers: you'll be able to either call up a movie for, let's say $2.50 *without* any ads, and view it as you wish, fast-forwarding whenever you want, or get it at a reduced rate *with* ads for $1.25. The only catch is that you won't be able to fast-forward the ads; they will come only in play mode (although you could use the ad-time to do much needed things like make a sandwich or go to the john, like in the old days of TV commercials). Alternatively, you may be able to see the movie for free—all you would have to do is answer 15 questions about some product, and they would get to use whatever information you provided.

But Stargazer will not just be limited to watching videos. Soon, shopping at your favorite stores from the comfort of your home will only be a click away. So will the stores' ability to know where you've browsed and what you've decided to buy. And as you browse through various ads, an icon will appear on the screen that, at the press of a button, will give you more information about a particular product and how to order it. No longer will you need to go to a store to be tempted by "impulse buys." No. These temptations will now be able to lure you right in your own home. One consumer was horrified at the prospect: "I don't want that [the temptation to impulse-buy] to happen. I hope that that's not going to be the case. It would distress me completely that they would start hitting you and hitting children with such incredible advertising."

The Stargazer system is billed as the "business of who's watching." It was set up to track the behavior of all viewers, permitting the development of customized commercials targeted to specific individuals: "the consumer has to self-identify." The response to this was simply, "Somewhere in your computer you will know the movies I've seen, the clothes I've bought, the ads I've seen, and how long I've lingered. Somewhere in your computer you will know more about me than even the government, than maybe even my wife. Shouldn't I be a little frightened to let you have so much information?" You be the judge.

Credit Records and Reporting Agencies

Most of us have encountered times when obtaining credit was essential before purchasing a car, a house, furniture, a vacation, or some other major item. Nor can many of us imagine life without the convenience of credit cards. Credit-reporting agencies, or credit bureaus, offer a valuable service in that they provide a record of your creditworthiness, which enables you to obtain credit when you need it. And everyone wants to have a good credit rating. If lenders couldn't make good credit decisions from an accurate assessment of your past credit performance, a high number of loans would fall into arrears, and ultimately payment would be defaulted. If that happened, the cost of such losses would eventually be borne by all consumers, in higher prices and higher charges for credit. In a credit economy, the existence of credit bureaus is essential to keep down the cost of credit by accurately maintaining records of your creditworthiness.

Credit files typically include records of your credit transactions, your payment history (on time, late once, consistently late), social security number, occupation, income, mortgage records, liens against you, bankruptcies, family information, date of birth, current and previous addresses, and telephone number. With so much sensitive information in one place, accuracy is paramount. Errors do creep in, however, and incorrect assumptions are made on the basis of faulty data. Even when mistakes are corrected, they can have an effect long afterward, as the following example shows.

> A person who is in the middle of a dispute with a key credit grantor, such as a mortgage lender, and who has stopped sending monthly payments pending resolution of the dispute, could be targeted by the credit bureau databanks during a risk assessment sweep as a likely future deadbeat. When this information is broadcast to all of his other creditors, a domino effect occurs. A black mark stains his accounts, resulting in untold harassment, and the loss of credit privileges each time he's just a day or two late paying his bills.[17]

Partly in response to such criticism and in an effort to develop better business practices, the larger credit bureaus such as Equifax have developed their own privacy codes, which among other things permit consumers to see their credit files and correct errors. Equifax's booklet, *Consumer Information and Privacy,* begins by enumerating the rights of individuals, including their right to privacy. This is followed by a section that reflects how these rights are implemented in practice. The list of practices is preceded by: "The following actions and initiatives have been undertaken to enhance privacy protection, improve information privacy, and provide professional services to consumers."

John Baker, former senior vice president of Equifax, also recognized the importance of privacy. "Social responsibility in the information age is everyone's business," he said. "In the information industry, it means maintaining the delicate balance between meeting the legitimate information needs of business and respecting the consumers' right to privacy." Equifax has a corporate statement of Fair Information Practices, including one that will assume greater importance with the arrival of the information highway: everyone is entitled to have his or her privacy "safeguarded through secure storage and careful transmittal of information." Addressing the importance of security in storing and transmitting information is a welcome addition to a voluntary code. Veronica Maidman, president and chief operating officer of Equifax Canada, says, "The tremendous advantages offered by such new technologies as the information highway cannot be exploited unless we address the very real concerns consumers have about the impact of technology on privacy."

Developing voluntary privacy codes is certainly a step in the right direction, but it might not be enough. Credit-reporting practices in the United States are regulated by the Fair Credit Reporting Act, while in Canada they are regulated provincially by consumer-reporting acts, yet these do not contain protections equal to privacy laws. Credit-reporting laws theoretically permit credit information to be disclosed only to prescribed parties such as employers and insurance companies or businesses with permissible purposes (such as credit evaluation or granting of licenses). Consequently, there is a lot of room for maneuvering. For example, credit information can be shared widely with uncategorized parties who have "other business needs involving a transaction with a consumer" or "business transactions involving consumers."

Violations of the Fair Credit Reporting Act are reportedly common. At the congressional hearings held in the United States in 1990 on the subject of tightening oversight of credit bureaus, Representative Charles Schumer commented on the practice of exploiting the weaknesses of the Fair Credit Reporting Act: "I am particularly troubled that certain credit bureaus have sought to create and exploit loopholes in the Fair Credit Reporting Act to expand the uses to which they can put credit information. Business by loophole, particularly in an area as sensitive as the privacy of credit information, is intolerable."

We think your best protection in this area is awareness. Make sure you know what's in your credit records and that the information accurately reflects your creditworthiness. Go to your credit bureau and ask to see your file. Ask questions about anything you don't understand. Bring any errors to the attention of the staff and ask that they be corrected. Then go back later and make sure that they have been corrected. It takes time, but it's worth the trouble.

Concluding Thought

Become an informed consumer. Raise your privacy awareness. Equip yourself with the knowledge you need. Speak
up, ask questions, be cautious, but most of all, don't just
passively give away your personal information. Take control of your information. Take control of your privacy.

Endnotes

1. Oscar Gandy, *The Panoptic Sort: A Political Economy of Personal Information* (Boulder: Westview Press, 1993), p. 140.

2. Evan Hendricks, "Latest Poll Shows Public Concern over Privacy Continues to Surge," *Privacy Times*, November 19, 1991, p. 7.

3. Ekos Research Associates, *Executive Summary to Privacy Revealed: The Canadian Privacy Survey* (Ekos Research Associates, Inc., 1993).

4. Gandy, *Panoptic Sort*, p. 220.

5. Anne Wells Branscomb, *Who Owns Information? From Privacy to Public Access* (New York: Basic Books, 1994), p. 28.

6. Gandy, *Panoptic Sort*, p. 221.

7. *USA Today*, October 24, 1995.

8. Gandy, *Panoptic Sort*, p. 143.

9. Branscomb, *Who Owns Information?* p. 29.

10. *Gandy*, Panoptic Sort, p. 187.

11. "Privacy: Junk-Mail Hater Seeks Profits from Sale of His Name," *Wall Street Journal*, October 13, 1995.

12. Lawrence Hunter and James B. Rule, "Toward Property Rights in Personal Information," paper presented to the Information and Privacy Commission, Ontario, December 17, 1993.

13. Eli Noam, "Privacy in Telecommunications: Markets, Rights, and Ethics in Telecommunications Regulations," in *Ethics in Telecommunications* (Cleveland: Office of the United Church of Christ, 1994).

14. Noam, "Privacy in Telecommunications," pp. 73–74.

15. David B. Hack, Congressional Research Service, Library of Congress, Washington, D.C., December 10, 1991, IB90085, p. CRS-9, in David H. Flaherty, "Telecommunications Privacy: A Report to the CRTC," May 1, 1992, p. 108.

16. Robert Ellis Smith, *Privacy Journal*, Vol. 21, No. 1 (November 1994).

17. Jeffrey Rothfedder, *Privacy for Sale: How Computerization Has Made Everyone's Private Life an Open Secret* (New York: Simon & Schuster, 1992), pp. 32–33.

Medical Privacy: How Safe Are Your Records?

I just didn't want to go public now because I'm not sick. I wanted to protect the privacy of my family. As of this moment, my life is going to change. I will deal with it because I know how to adapt. But it's wearying to have to fight misconceptions and the ignorance that people have about this disease.

ARTHUR ASHE, UPON HAVING HIS HIV STATUS MADE PUBLIC

Contrary to Popular Belief

Most people think their medical records are strongly protected. They are not. In a 1993 Louis Harris poll in the United States, 85 percent of respondents felt that protecting medical confidentiality was very important, and 67 percent thought there were strong confidentiality laws on the books. In fact, only seven states have such laws. You probably expect that your most sensitive personal information, ranging from treatment sought for impotence, to psychiatric counseling, to a variety of test results, is protected as strongly as Fort Knox. It is not. You probably also believe that your innermost thoughts and fears, or medical conditions that you may not wish to share with anyone else, not even your family, remain the exclusive domain of confidential communications between you and your doctor. They do not.

Here are some common myths about your medical records:

1. Strong laws are in place to safeguard the confidentiality of your medical information.

2. When you go to a hospital, no one other than your medical team has access to your records.

3. When you pour your heart out to your psychiatrist every week, no one else can ever read his or her notes about you.

Medical privacy laws are some of the weakest around. In the United States, there is no federal law for medical privacy, and the small number of state laws that protect medical records vary considerably in their scope and coverage. As law professor Paul Schwartz, an expert on privacy laws, states, "The present regulatory scheme in the United States consists of federal law that applies only to data in the control of the government or to certain, specific kinds of health data. The regulatory scheme also includes state measures that create a patchwork of insufficient protection." What's more, state laws tend to favor disclosure of information rather than privacy protection.

Numerous observers, from the Privacy Protection Study Commission in 1977 to the Office of Technology Assessment in 1993, have commented on the lack of protection for privacy in health care information. What is perhaps the most harmful to privacy is the secondary use and disclosure of medical information, unknown to the data subject. A lot of people besides health care providers have access to your medical records. Furthermore, when patients request access to their records, it is often denied.

The picture is not much better in Canada. As in the United States, there is no federal medical privacy law. Although the Federal Privacy Act protects medical records falling under its jurisdiction, most places where such records reside either are regulated provincially (hospitals) or are found in the private sector (doctors' offices, laboratories). Except in Quebec, provincial privacy laws do not extend to the private sector, where most medical records are found. In some provinces, however, such as British Columbia and Alberta, privacy laws do cover records held by hospitals.

In Ontario, a province with privacy legislation, the law does not apply to hospitals, even though less sensitive personal information held by the province is strongly protected by this law. This makes no sense. From day 1, the Ontario information and privacy commissioner has lobbied the government strongly to provide much-needed privacy protection for all medical records, regardless of where they may be found. Although great strides were made in 1991 toward developing a comprehensive access and privacy law for the province, in the years that followed, the government's priorities turned elsewhere. To this day, hospital records do not fall under the existing privacy law, nor is there comparable protection for private sector organizations.

In 1980, Horace Krever, then judge of the Ontario High Court of Justice, issued his report on the results of the commission he had headed to inquire into the confidentiality of health information. Justice Krever chronicled a litany of security leaks and privacy violations, ranging from private investigators impersonating hospital staff to gain access to patient charts, to poor procedural controls that could have prevented such abuses. Privacy Commissioner David Flaherty has referred to this inquiry as revealing the worst instances of systemic abuses of privacy in the Western world. Although it is far from being the only documentation of unauthorized access to confidential records, it is one of the most compelling. The initial narrow scope of the inquiry was expanded considerably when the extent of the problems was realized.

The report contains 170 recommendations for much-needed reform, including the need to develop comprehensive legislation governing the protection and security of health records. While everyone appeared to be disturbed by the findings, and the recommendations were duly studied by successive governments, 15 years later, they have yet to be acted upon. This is not to say that reforms have not been introduced in hospitals. But whether these policies are sufficient is open to question, as is the degree of consistency among measures adopted in various hospitals. There are documented inconsistencies in granting patients access to their files and in the fees charged for such access. A survey conducted by the Patients' Rights Association even found that access policies could be inconsistent from one department to another within the same hospital.

In addition, it was pointed out that in most cases, the primary care physician had to be notified of a patient's request to see his or her file before such access was granted. Mary Margaret Steckle, executive director of the Patients' Rights Association, told us that this practice often causes patients a great deal of concern, enough at times to withdraw the request for access because they're so worried about how it might look to their doctor, in whose hands their medical fate lies. She said, "In light of the fact that patients feel vulnerable and powerless in these situations, they have no wish to take any action that may alienate their physician or cause problems in their patient-doctor relationship."

Equally questionable are the policies (where they exist) governing the use and disclosure of medical records and test results. Who beyond your doctor is permitted access to your files? Is your information ever disclosed to third parties outside the hospital? If so, have you been advised of these practices? Was your consent ever obtained? Were you ever consulted? The majority of complaints that the Patients' Rights Association receives are related to patients' limited access to their medical records and unauthorized disclosures of information contained in their records. Vast numbers of people may have access to your hospital records—your primary care physician, specialists, nurses, nursing assistants, administrators, lab technicians, residents, medical students, and clerical staff. Patients are generally not advised of these practices, and their consent is rarely sought.

And very often, contact with each of these medical personnel generates some type of record, in either electronic or paper form. When added to other records that have accumulated over years of contact with the health care system through doctors, pharmacies, laboratories, clinics, and other health professionals, as well as public and private insurers, the files pile up. With the increasing ease of access to information (both authorized and unauthorized) via networked communications and developments on the information highway, the threats to your privacy are mounting.

Video Records Have More Protection

The U.S. Video Privacy Protection Act protects the confidentiality of your video rental records. While it may be laudable that your private viewing habits are afforded the protection of law, the absence of such protection for your medical records stands sharply in contrast. Surely the intimate details contained in your medical records should be afforded the same degree of protection. As Sheri Alpert notes, "As the law now stands, while the unauthorized disclosure of medical records may be ethically reprehensible, in the majority of states in this country, it is not illegal."

In the 1992 case of *McInerney v. MacDonald*, the Supreme Court of Canada ruled that in the absence of legislation, patients were entitled to view and, for a reasonable fee, obtain copies of all the information in their medical files that a physician had considered in giving advice or treatment. Access to medical records may be denied on a limited basis if it is believed that such access may result in mental or physical harm to the patient. However, the patient may appeal the decision if a physician denies access; it is up to the physician to justify the denial.

Remember, just one inaccuracy in the information contained in your records, be they credit records or medical records, can have profound ramifications. For one woman, inaccurate medical records resulted in her receiving improper treatment, which had a debilitating effect on her health. In a submission to the Ontario Legislative Assembly during its 1994 review of the privacy law, Ms. C. strongly encouraged the government to extend the law to apply to hospitals. She had repeatedly failed in her attempts to have her records corrected. "Correcting a medical record should be as simple as correcting a credit record," she said. "It should be a matter of evidence....The hospital refused to address [the misdiagnosis]. It...repeatedly did not address my request for a correction, despite the evidence supplied; and finally told me [in writing] to go to another hospital if I didn't like 'care' like this....I'm sure you'll agree this is no way to treat a sick person, but there's no law against it."[1] Without any privacy laws that extend to hospitals, and with no privacy commissioner to turn to for appeal, Ms. C. had no recourse but to accept the hospital's dismissal of her complaint as unfounded.

It Could Happen to You

Even in the province with the greatest privacy protection, Quebec, unauthorized disclosures of medical records occur. A Montreal woman who had just returned from a hospital stay after being diagnosed with cancer received a phone solicitation from a local funeral home; the funeral home asked for her by name, although she had an unlisted number. After much pressing, the salesperson admitted that he had been given her number by someone from the hospital. Under Quebec's Privacy Law, the woman is suing both the hospital and the funeral home for infringing on her private life and not respecting the confidentiality of her medical records. Upon investigation, neither the Quebec Privacy Commission nor the hospital could determine who had been responsible for the release of the woman's medical information, other than to narrow it down to three large departments.[2]

It Happened to Her: Nydia Velazquez

During my campaign for Congress, I realized that no one is immune to privacy violations. I had my private, personal medical records leaked to the newspapers in New York City....Just imagine what I felt, three weeks after I won this victory in the primary, when I woke up one morning with a phone call from my friend Peter Hamill, a reporter at the *New York Post*. He told me that the night before, the *Post* had received an anonymous fax of my records from St. Claire Hospital. The records showed that I had been admitted to the hospital a year ago, seeking medical assistance for a suicide attempt. He told me that other newspapers across the city had received the same information and the *New York Post* was going to run a front-page story the next day....When I found out this information was being published in the newspaper and that I had no power to stop it, I felt violated. I trusted the system, and it failed me. —Testimony of Representative Nydia Velazquez to the Senate Judiciary Committee, 1994

Your worst fear comes true—your failed suicide attempt a year earlier appears on the front page of the major newspapers, shortly after you have beaten the odds and won a seat in Congress. One can only imagine how Representative Nydia Velazquez felt upon learning that the most intimate details of her life in seeking medical treatment would soon become public knowledge. Little could she have predicted such an outcome, because like countless others, she had trusted the system. "I went to the hospital confident that I would receive treatment and that my experience would be private, between me and my doctor....Very few people knew about my situation, and I made the decision of not sharing it with my family."

Your medical history should be your business and yours alone, not to be used as a means by which to exploit you, or to discriminate against you. Fortunately, Ms. Velazquez received a great deal of support from friends and constituents alike who rallied around her. No doubt they too were shocked at the ease with which such sensitive medical information could be obtained from hospital records and released to unauthorized third parties (in this case, the press). Despite all the support she received, Ms. Velazquez says that she relives the pain and humiliation of this experience, over which she had absolutely no control, whenever she talks about it. We would not have presented Ms. Velazquez's story here without first having obtained her consent, which she kindly granted so that similar incidents could be prevented in the future.

It is interesting to note that after this disclosure of her medical records, Nydia Velazquez was approached by a number of people who feared that their own records involving visits for psychiatric treatment might also be made public. Needless to say, she could not put their fears to rest. Neither can we, because unauthorized disclosures of your medical records are not the only ones you have to worry about.

Government Audits Expose Patient Records

A physician's or psychiatrist's patient files may be opened up to many eyes during a government audit conducted to prevent fraud and fiscal abuse. In Ontario, under the Health Insurance Act, every insured person is deemed to have authorized his or her physician or other health care practitioner to provide information to the Ontario Health Insurance Plan (OHIP). According to Tracey Tremayne-Lloyd, a lawyer specializing in medical law, your files may be photocopied and distributed to various committees during such an audit. And you will never know, because you will never be told. Tremayne-Lloyd views this as an "unnecessary encroachment into the patient's privacy" that will not be remedied until the government changes its practices to reflect more sensitivity to the privacy rights of patients.[3]

A physician who is being audited is given a computer-generated list of up to 200 patients identified by name and with full identifying information, including the diagnosis and the nature of the services they received. The physician must make the records of those patients available to an inspector from OHIP. The inspector photocopies much of the records and includes them with the report that is sent to the Medical Review Committee of the College of Physicians and Surgeons. Through this route, sensitive medical information, including psychotherapy records, may be revealed to various levels of indiscriminating personnel. Tremayne-Lloyd states: "The patient's chart will be exposed to the inspector and his staff, and exposed to the members of the Medical Review Committee and their staff. This is to say nothing of the OHIP clerks who assembled all of the original data on the physician's patients in the first place."

If the physician is asked to attend a meeting of the review committee, another 100 patient records will be exposed to the members of the committee. The records are also exposed to the clerical staff at the college. If the physician appeals a decision, patient records will be further exposed to another round of people: to the members of the Health Services Appeal Board, the lawyers on both sides, any expert witnesses called to testify on behalf of the physician, and any witnesses OHIP may call. If this tribunal is unable to resolve the matter, the decision may be appealed to the Supreme Court of Ontario, at which time all the records enter into the public domain. "The patient records are now evidence in a legal proceeding," says Tremayne-Lloyd. "Anyone can walk down to the courthouse and examine them when this occurs. And more significant is the fact that the appeal is argued in open court and the content of the records have to be discussed in the course of the lawyers' argument."

There are sound reasons for conducting audits, but surely a process could be developed whereby patient records, when required by an inspector, could have the personal identifiers removed from the records prior to their photocopying and distribution to third parties. This is only one of a number of improvements that could be made to enhance privacy.

Take charge by becoming aware. Ask your doctor how he or she safeguards the confidentiality of your medical records, and whether others have ever had access to your records through an audit. As well, ask your doctor to notify you if such a situation ever arises, so that at the very least you will know what's going on, and you may have an opportunity to object. As Tremayne-Lloyd notes, "The patient has never been consulted, has never complained, and has no idea that his or her medical chart...is being exposed to all and sundry in this way."

Information Technology and Medical Records

As in other areas, information technology has made the speedy transmission of medical information to multiple parties much easier. In its study *Protecting Privacy in Computerized Medical Information,* the U.S. Office of Technology Assessment concluded that laws in the United States did not provide consistent or comprehensive protection for medical information. Recent proposals to computerize medical records in the United States and have them electronically linked through a single health card will greatly increase the number of people who will have access to your medical information without your consent. Growing networks and communication systems will compound the problem of disclosure. The Committee on Regional Health Data Networks of the Institute of Medicine noted that the "threats and potential harms" from such disclosures of medical information, "are real and not numerically trivial." Among the third parties that medical information might be circulated to are insurance companies, employers, pharmacies, health service providers, hospitals, public health agencies, administrators, social welfare programs, and direct marketers.

Yes, direct marketers. For how else would companies be able to compile lists of impotent middle-aged men, or elderly incontinent women? These are only a few of the available mailing lists that provide detailed information about people who have specific medical conditions. And it may be the case that you, through little choice of your own, have given this information to them. You may have been forced to consent to the release of your information for a wide variety of purposes. We say "forced" because when faced with dire consequences, such as being denied medical insurance, you have little real choice other than to consent to what is being asked of you. This type of consent is neither free nor informed, but is frequently obtained by having individuals sign broad release forms that permit wide-ranging secondary disclosures to third parties. As law professor Paul Schwarz points out, "Service payers such as insurance companies often have their customers, the future consumers of health care services, sign broad, "blanket" disclosure releases. Such documents have been used to justify almost any secondary use of medical data." This includes secondary disclosure to the Medical Information Bureau.

The Medical Information Bureau (MIB) is a large organization in Massachusetts that is supplied by insurance companies with the medical information of millions of Americans and Canadians. The MIB was formed as a repository for information to be exchanged by insurers to prevent insurance fraud through misreporting or concealing significant medical information. It has a membership of roughly 750 life insurance companies—almost all the major companies that issue life, health, or disability insurance in North America. Insurers rely on MIB files as a significant source of information.

The problem is, you don't know what information the MIB has in its files, and you don't know whether it's accurate. With medical summaries on more than 12 million people in the MIB database, it wouldn't be too hard to find a few mistakes, and the MIB makes no effort to verify any of the information reported to it. Erroneous medical information could then circulate widely through the electronic maze of networks and databases. What's more, the information in the MIB's files is not restricted to the medical. Information about any activity that might pose an insurance risk—a bad driving record, participation in hazardous sports, aviation activities—is also collected.

The only way that errors in the MIB's database will see the light of day is when you request a copy of your file and then challenge the MIB to correct the errors. Write to the Medical Information Bureau, P.O. Box 105, Essex Station, Boston, MA 02112. But be warned: one request to see a personal file never received a response from the MIB. We suspect that trying to correct personal information may be even more difficult. (If you decide to write, let us know what happens. We would appreciate hearing your stories.)

Laws Needed to Protect Medical Privacy

In light of the Clinton administration's goal of national health care reform, the need for a medical privacy law became more pressing. In 1994, a U.S. bill was introduced by Representative Gary Condit to develop Fair Information Practices for health care information, but it did not pass. Nor did a number of other bills aimed at data protection. In 1995 Senator Robert Bennett introduced another bill, the Medical Records Confidentiality Act. While there is widespread agreement that much-needed federal protection for health care records is long overdo, there appears to be little consensus as to how to achieve it. The aim of the bill is to introduce uniform federal rules for the use and disclosure of health care records: who would be permitted to see what, and under what circumstances.

Supporters of the Bennett bill argue that computerized medical records are now available to practically anyone who wants them, making the need to introduce some immediate protection imperative. Would having something put in place, no matter how flawed, be better than nothing? Many think not. Rather, the bill would simply serve as a smokescreen, giving the appearance of privacy protection for medical records when, in fact, it would legitimize their widespread disclosure.

Opponents of the Bennett bill (S. 1360) are numerous, ranging from patients' rights groups, the ACLU, the Electronic Privacy Information Center (EPIC), and the Consumer Project on Technology (CPT), to medical ethicists and academics. They argue that the bill's main objective is to create a framework within which patient-identified records could be given to various data collection agencies, without patient knowledge or consent. Under such a scheme, patients would have little control over who would see their medical records because their specific, informed consent would not be required. Obtaining your consent before the release of your medical information by a trusted party (your doctor) is an important means of ensuring confidentiality. This would essentially disappear. It would become much easier for large companies to create massive databases containing your medical information.

James Love, Director of the CPT at the Center for the Study of Responsive Law, a Ralph Nader group based in Washington, thinks that the Bennett bill is fundamentally flawed: "As introduced, S. 1360 does more to protect the medical records industry than the privacy of patients. The legislation severely limits state action on medical records privacy issues."[4] He is not alone.

Dr. Denise Nagel, a psychiatrist and executive director of the Coalition for Patient Rights, has taken the extreme measure of advising her patients not to seek reimbursement from their insurance companies because psychiatric records would no longer remain private. "This bill would actually legislate patient confidentiality out of existence," she cautioned.[5] Professor

Lawrence Gostin, director of the Law and Public Health Program at Georgetown University, said that the Bennett bill not only doesn't protect privacy, but is misleading in both its name and intent: "We need a privacy law, but one that protects the confidentiality of patients. We don't have that now, and this bill is not going to give it to us. It's a false promise."[6] George Annas, health law professor at Boston University, suggested that the bill should be renamed "the databank efficiency act of 1995."[7]

Clearly, a federal medical privacy law is needed, but at what cost? While some new protections would be introduced by the Bennett bill and a right of access to one's medical records created (only about half the states presently provide such a right), confidentiality may disappear in the process. Do you really want untold numbers of strangers looking at your most sensitive information—your medical records? We think that forfeiting confidentiality is too high a price to pay, and so do most Americans. A 1993 Harris poll found that 85 percent of Americans felt that protecting the confidentiality of their medical records was "absolutely essential" or "very important." We think you would agree.

Basic Security Measures

Here is an example of how important basic security measures can be, and how technology is not the only threat to your privacy; good old-fashioned lack of common sense can result in a lot of damage as well.

The administrator of a hospital in Bella Bella, Canada ordered that hospital records that were scheduled for destruction be burned on the beach. Ordinarily, such sensitive personal records would be shredded or incinerated. Eight boxes of confidential medical records were set on fire, whereupon along came the local fire department and quickly doused the flames: fires are not allowed on public beaches. The soggy documents were soon carried out by the tide, and later washed up along the shoreline. The British Columbia (B.C.) Freedom of Information and Privacy Association called this "notorious" incident the worst privacy "fiasco" it had ever encountered: "People who helped scavenge the records were astonished to find all manner of their neighbors' medical records and even adoption documents."[8] At the time of this incident, B.C.'s privacy law did not cover hospital records (they do now). But Privacy Commissioner Flaherty took immediate action to ensure that the Ministry of Health's investigation of this matter took into account the privacy issues. The commissioner continues to monitor the ministry's implementation of the measures identified in the report. Hospitals are now required to protect personal information records by instituting reasonable security measures. This particular incident is not representative of how most public bodies dispose of their records, but it does underscore the importance and need for proper information management practices, as well as secure disposal techniques.

Genetic Privacy and Your DNA

An extension of medical privacy is genetic privacy, which involves your ability to maintain control over your genetic information—your genetic makeup. Like other types of technology, genetic testing, which will one day identify all of our genes, is a two-edged sword.

Every one of our cells contains DNA, or deoxyribonucleic acid, the building block of our chromosomes. Each human cell contains 46 chromosomes, 23 from the mother paired with 23 from the father. Arranged in these 23 pairs of chromosomes are an estimated 100,000 genes, which are like sets of instructions at the molecular level that direct human growth, similar to the blueprints for a house. In this way, children inherit certain physical and behavioral characteristics from their parents and pass them on to their own children. Because of the minute size of these genes, identifying them is a very difficult task; only about 5 percent of the chromosomal locations of all human genes have been discovered to date.

The Human Genome Project, possibly the largest research project in the world, is a concerted effort by research teams all over the world to identify which genes are responsible for causing what traits and conditions. (The term *genome* refers to the complete set of genetic information, in its entirety.) The research undertaken in this project will eventually map the location of all genes along the chromosomes where they are found.

Genes responsible for muscular dystrophy, cystic fibrosis, Tay-Sachs disease, Huntington's disease, breast cancer, and many other disorders have already been discovered. One day it will be possible to map all of our genetically determined characteristics, both physical and mental. The medical benefits of such discoveries speak for themselves. We are all aware of them.

Less aware are we of the threats to privacy that are sure to arise in this area. The secondary uses of information resulting from genetic testing will be many if left unchecked and unregulated. Indeed, there may be no area in greater need of Fair Information Practices.

> Imagine a society where the government had samples of tissue and fluid from the entire community on file and a computerized databank of each individual's DNA profile. Imagine then that not only law enforcement officials but insurance companies, employers, schools, adoption agencies, and many other organizations could gain access to those files on a "need to know" basis or on a showing that access is "in the public interest." Imagine then that an individual could be turned down for jobs, insurance, adoption, health care, and other social services and benefits on the basis of information contained in her DNA profile, such as genetic disease, heritage, or someone else's subjective idea of a genetic "flaw."[9]

In the haste to use this new-found information, it may be forgotten that many genes reveal only a predisposition to a particular condition, which may or may not materialize. A host of other factors, ranging from diet to stress, will combine forces to shape the final outcome—not genes alone.

Preserving your genetic privacy, or the right to control the uses of your genetic information, will be extremely important, and perhaps extremely difficult, given the anticipated demand for your information by third parties such as employers and insurers. And herein lies one of the greatest threats to privacy from information arising out of genetic testing—the use of this information for purposes unrelated to the original medical reason. The prospect of using genetic test results as a screening technique in the workplace could lead to a new form of discrimination—one that may create an entire class of "unemployable" people. Likewise, some fear that the use of genetic tests by insurers may lead to a class of "uninsurable" people. We talk of "classes" and not individuals because, with the inherited nature of genetic traits, "undesirable" traits will follow people like scarlet letters, handed down from generation to generation. Thus, losing your genetic privacy has implications not simply for yourself but also for your children, and their children. As Anthony Gottlieb writes:

> Beware of geneticists bearing discoveries. Their findings, perhaps more than any others in science, are likely to be abused and harmfully misinterpreted in the near future. Danger usually comes from wherever you are not looking. Everybody is ready for the mutant viruses, plants, and two-headed chimpanzees to crawl out of the ventilation shafts of biotechnology laboratories. That is not where the problem will come from. Everybody knows about the blue-eyed "designer babies" who will be born quoting Aristotle. But they are not the real danger either. Look instead at insurance companies, personnel departments, in the health pages of next year's women's magazines. That is where the trouble is brewing.[10]

In addition, there is the question of data collection and the development of DNA databases. Some would say this should be permitted, that the forensic use of DNA for identification is no different from using and keeping identifiable fingerprints on file. But will there be calls for various *groups* (recipients of social assistance, say, or immigrants) to be DNA-printed, as there have been calls for them to be fingerprinted?

When all human genes have been identified and their locations known, when the information highway is up and running, the convergence of these two technologies will permit you to do what is now impossible. Dr. Martin Moskovits, professor of chemistry, put it this way: "All you will have to do is take a hangnail and drop it into a test tube at your local laboratory, where they will have it tested and your genetic map computed. This will result in a telephone book of output, which can be sent to you electronically via networks. Just turn on your computer and call up the program that will make sense of the meaningless stream of DNA sequences; then select what you want to know from the menu." Do you possess the gene for alcoholism or depression? Do you have any interesting personality genes? How smart are you? Or do the same with your spouse's genetic code and combine it with your own—check out the odds of your children having blond hair and blue eyes, being tall, or being prone to depression, alcoholism, or heart disease.

Will it become desirable to select our mates only after reviewing their genetic profile? Will we one day be able to design our children to suit our particular tastes, just as we select the color and style of a suit? But do we really want to reduce childbirth to a checkoff process? And the question of who ultimately gets to decide cannot be avoided. Will it be everyone for herself, or will there be mounting pressure to reject all but the most genetically desirable offspring? We would all like to see an end to debilitating diseases such as Tay-Sachs or thalassemia, which are fatal at an early age, but where will we draw the line? At Down's syndrome? Diabetes? Allergies? Homosexuality? We need think back only 50 years to the Third Reich and its experiments with eugenics. Are we in danger of seeing history too easily repeat itself? These are only a few of the many profound ethical and social issues that must be grappled with.

Biotechnology

One more area we should bring to your attention is biotechnology, which involves the interplay of technology and biological organisms to harness the uses of a host of microorganisms, presumably for the advancement of society. It involves the use of biological processes and living cells to manufacture new products. But like any new technology, it needs to be explored from an ethical and social perspective before we rush into it. Public education about a broad range of issues involved in biotechnology will be needed before there can be any consumer confidence in the safety of the resulting products. Many questions must be asked and fears dispelled regarding the potential adverse effects of biotechnology.

While Professor Moskovits views biotechnology as one of the most important technological advances in the history of humankind, he notes that "in making slaves of bacteria, it can also make monsters." Genetic alteration and manipulation require careful study, followed closely by regulated controls. While the commercialization of life forms goes beyond our present discussion of privacy, it is based on genetic forms of engineering, which are by no means restricted to lower life forms or animals. Genetic engineering may be benign or potentially harmful. We must proceed with caution. Some fear the emergence of a new eugenics movement, fueled by the use of new discoveries in the field of genetics. One can only imagine the horrors of such a prospect.

Concluding Thought

The sensitive information contained in your medical records should receive the highest degree of protection possible: protection from unauthorized disclosure, protection from direct marketers, protection from prying eyes. But this is not presently the case. If you want it to change, start asking questions and write to your political representative. If you've ever been a patient and value your privacy, it might be worth the effort.

Endnotes

1. Ms. C., "Submission to the Standing Committee of the [Ontario] Legislative Assembly at Hearings on the Freedom of Information and Privacy Act, January 20, 1994, pp. 4–5.

2. Evan Hendricks, *Privacy Times*, Vol. 14, No. 12 (June 20, 1994).

3. Tracey Tremayne-Lloyd, "Access and Privacy of Health Care Information," paper presented at McMaster University Hospital, Hamilton, Ontario, June 17, 1994.

4. James P. Love, "Submission to the Senate Committee on Labor and Human Resources," November 14, 1995. S. 1360 Hearings held by Nancy Kassenbaum.

5. Gina Kolata, "When Patients' Records Are Commodities for Sale," *New York Times*, November 15, 1995.

6. Ibid.

7. Ibid.

8. British Columbia Freedom of Information and Privacy Association, "Bungled Bonfire of Medical Records Fuels Call for Records Protection Law," *FIPA Bulletin* (Fall 1994).

9. Janet C. Hoeffel, "The Dark Side of DNA Profiling: Unreliable Scientific Evidence Meets the Criminal Defendant," *Stanford Law Review*, Vol. 42, No. 465 (1990), pp. 533–534; quoted in *Genetic Testing and Privacy* (Ottawa: Privacy Commissioner of Canada, 1992).

10. Anthony Gottlieb, "Are Your Genes Up to Scratch?" *The World in 1991* (1990), p. 18; quoted in *Genetic Testing and Privacy*.

Workplace Privacy: Does It Exist?

It doesn't matter whether you work in a factory, in an office, or as a highly paid engineer or professional—you are very likely under observation, with or without your permission, in some way by computers or machines controlled by your boss.

MICHELLE JANKANISH
ILO Workers' Privacy Report, 1993

Perhaps more than any other area, privacy in the workplace generates a great deal of controversy. Some argue that you should check your privacy at the door when you go to work. After all, your employer hired you to do a job and to perform the services for which you are paid; your employer surely has the right to monitor your performance. But does that mean you should completely abandon your right to privacy at the workplace, or that your employer has the right to monitor those of your activities not related, or only peripherally related, to your employment, either on or off the job?

The expectation of privacy in the workplace may not be the same as elsewhere, but it does not disappear. Why not? Because your employer's need to monitor your performance and have access to information about you must legitimately be related to employment purposes.

Employee Monitoring: Surveillance on the Job

There is a long tradition of employers watching over employees to supervise their activities. Today's advancing technologies permit a far greater ability to monitor employees electronically and to probe more deeply into their lives. Computers, massive databases, networked communications, listening devices, and video cameras all make it easier to monitor employees' actions, sometimes covertly. Technological advances may allow the boss to watch more closely than ever before, but it is not clear how effective such techniques may actually be in enhancing performance and advancing the bottom line. Some would argue that these activities are generally counter-productive, accomplishing the opposite of what was intended by increasing levels of stress and decreasing motivation and trust. The potential negative impact resulting from a loss of privacy in the workplace is described in a Privacy Commission report:

> Central to the issues of workplace privacy for employees are feelings related to dignity, trust, respect, autonomy, and individuality. When invasions of privacy occur, employees often feel that self-worth, morale, and the overall quality of working life are eroded. The ensuing negative impact of invasions of privacy on work quality and productivity is hidden human and real costs (e.g., absenteeism and employees' compensation claims), not often calculated by employers.[1]

Efficiency Versus Privacy: Must They Be at Odds?

Must we sacrifice privacy in the pursuit of efficiency? Most employee monitoring is done in the name of efficiency—to increase levels of productivity. But whether it achieves this goal is questionable. Some studies have shown that employees experience higher rates of both physical and psychological problems in the presence of relentless monitoring.[2] Put yourself in the following real-life workplace, a company that processes responses to direct-mail ads, and ask whether your performance would be improved. Try to imagine working in this atmosphere:

> The employees, who make $6 an hour, work at their computers under rigid supervision. The office windows are covered, to prevent distraction. Conversation unrelated to busi-

ness is forbidden. Desks all face in the same direction, toward a pedestal where a boss stands like a schoolmaster. Other supervisors watch the workers from behind, and eight TV cameras are always ready to zoom in on one desk and spot any infraction of the rule.[3]

Employer scrutiny has been broadened by computers and their ability to collect and analyze vast amounts of personal information, held in numerous databases, linked together to form a detailed profile. Professor Andrew Clement, who specializes in the social impact of new technologies, warns that these "fine-grained profiles of individual employee behavior...can be used in situations far from what was originally expected. In an informational sense, the workplace becomes transparent, with virtually everything one does potentially on view by others. Metaphorically, it could become like working in a 'fishbowl.'"[4] It is this transparency of our lives to our employers that is cause for concern. How we live our lives outside the workplace should not be our employers' business unless it has a direct bearing on the job. Even when this is clearly the case, as with safety-sensitive jobs (airplane pilots, truck drivers), direct performance-related measures are considered to be more effective in determining our suitability to perform the required tasks. This must be the reason for employers wishing to seek personal information about their employees, not the desire to peer into their personal lives.

Direct performance-related measures tend to be the best indicators of whether an employee can perform assigned duties. The problem with indirect measures, in the form of a growing list of surveillance techniques, is that they often don't work. If the boss wants to know if someone is impaired on the job, that's where the boss should test and what the boss should test for. But this is not often the case. Law professor Bruce Feldthusen refers to drug testing as "lifestyle control." "It has nothing to do with productivity or employer interests. None of these tests tell you anything about whether or not this person is impaired at work."[5]

Beyond assessing your performance on the job, your employer should not have the right to additional nonoccupational information—an intrusion upon an employee's legitimate right to privacy in and out of the workplace. Otherwise, far too much of your personal information could become accessible: "The potential exists for employers to know about all aspects of their employees' lives including their health, genetic and psychological makeup, finances, schooling, past experience, how they spend their private time, and how they behave in the workplace from minute to minute. In effect, employees may become transparent to their employers."[6] With such transparency comes loss of control over your personal information, your actions, and your private life.

The difficult question, as always, is where to draw the line. Technological advances are steadily extending that line further and further, permitting greater encroachment into the sphere of privacy you should legitimately be entitled to in the workplace. Electronic sweatshop or fishbowl—neither is desirable; neither should be acceptable.

Every Move You Make: Video Surveillance

Take, for example, video cameras in the workplace—in the washrooms, to be exact, or in locker rooms where people change into their work clothes, or in similar areas where employees should reasonably have an expectation of privacy. Twenty employees, male and female, took their employer to court over precisely this type of surveillance. The employer, a power company in West Virginia, felt it had the right to videotape its employees anywhere it wanted in the workplace. The state court did not agree. The employees were successful in obtaining a permanent injunction against their employer and were awarded $80,000 in damages.

Whether video surveillance is used for legitimate security purposes or for monitoring the job performance of employees, its all-embracing sweep leaves no action uncaptured, not even those that are totally unrelated to the job. Because video surveillance casts such a wide net, it gathers information well beyond that related to work performance and observes people

without any suspicion of wrongdoing. Since this form of surveillance is so invasive and may capture actions unrelated to
the job, it should not be conducted covertly. Employees should
be told that it is taking place and told why.

Technological solutions may form part of the answer in alert-
ing workers to various types of electronic monitoring. For example, a faint tone accompanying telephone monitoring would let
employees know when their calls were being monitored. A visual
signal on a computer screen could indicate that one's electronic
files had been entered. In the case of video surveillance, a monitor that continuously displays what is being viewed would serve
as a reminder of the presence of the cameras.

Employee Testing: Drugs, HIV, Genetic Testing

The expectation of physical privacy at the workplace is another murky area. Should employers be permitted to demand
bodily fluids from their employees for testing, or to obtain the
results of medical tests for such conditions as HIV status or
the presence of a cancer gene—that is, tests not conducted
for employment purposes? Some say that with the *consent* of
the employee, such testing and access to test results should be
an acceptable practice in the workplace. Yet the word "consent" in the context of the workplace, which tends to be characterized by an imbalance of power between employer and
employee, is virtually stripped of any meaning. Few employees
are in a position to deny consent when they know that doing
so could jeopardize their prospects for advancement, and job
applicants would view saying no as a barrier to getting the job.
In such cases, consent should be viewed as neither informed
nor freely obtained, rendering it of little value. Indeed, the
Australian Privacy Charter states that "consent is meaningless
where people have no option but to consent in order to obtain
a benefit or a service."

A growing trend among employers is the intrusive practice
of subjecting employees and job candidates to drug testing,
whereby a urine specimen is obtained and analyzed for the

presence of illicit drugs. Drug testing is becoming especially common in the United States; its use in Canada also appears to be increasing. The privacy commissioner issued a comprehensive report, *Drug Testing and Privacy,* in 1990, that contained 20 recommendations for the use of drug testing, which, in most cases, involves urinalysis. To prevent the employee from tampering or making substitutions, the sample is sometimes taken while others observe. Aside from their intrusiveness, such tests tend to have error rates up to 40 percent. The other major problem with them is that they detect not only illicit drugs but legitimate ones too (prescription and over-the-counter drugs), as well as alcohol consumed within the previous few days. As the privacy commissioner noted, "Urinalysis can indicate only that a person has consumed a drug [illicit or licit] within the recent past....At best, a person who tests "positive" for drug use may have been impaired at some past time. One cannot confirm, however, that the person was impaired....Urinalysis cannot determine precisely when the drug was used....Nor can it identify the quantity of the drug ingested."[7]

It would seem to be of little value to an employer to know that an employee had consumed some substance, including medications or alcohol, at some time before the test. Is this useful in assessing on-the-job performance or inferring, as one bank hinted, an employee's trustworthiness? The Canadian Civil Liberties Association, represented by general counsel Alan Borovoy, took the Toronto Dominion Bank to court over its mandatory drug-testing policy. The Canadian Human Rights Tribunal ruled that the bank's policy did not constitute discrimination under the Human Rights Act; the Civil Liberties Association has appealed. In any case, the decision cannot be viewed as an endorsement of drug testing. Quite the contrary, it contained a mixed message.

As Max Yalden, the Canadian human rights commissioner, put it, "It's kind of like two judgments. Up to a certain point, they seem to be saying what the bank did was all right; then they get around to examining the substance of the policy, and from that point on they really slam it."[8]

From a privacy perspective, the ruling was quite favorable, in that it did not support a blanket mandatory policy for drug testing. It referred to the practice of requiring urine specimens as "a major step in the invasion of privacy of many individuals in the employment field." Borovoy said, "The paramount issue here is the substantial and needless invasion of employee privacy. A urine test tells you a lot about a person's lifestyle and tells you virtually nothing about the person's ability to do the job."

The case was appealed to the Federal Court of Canada. On April 24, 1996, Justice Sandra Simpson ordered that the earlier decision be set aside. The case has been sent back to the Human Rights Tribunal to determine whether a clear link can be made between a positive drug test and job performance. If the two cannot be found to be "rationally related," then the Federal Court has directed the Tribunal to find that the drug-testing policy contravenes the Canadian Human Rights Act.

On that basis, drug testing should be used only in very limited circumstances. The privacy commissioner has identified the conditions under which random mandatory drug testing of a group, "on the basis of behavioral patterns of the group as a whole," may be justifiable:

- There are reasonable grounds to believe that there is a significant prevalence of drug use or impairment within the group.
- The drug use or impairment poses a substantial threat to the safety of the public or other members of the group.
- The behavior of individuals in the group cannot otherwise be adequately supervised.
- There are reasonable grounds to believe that drug testing can significantly reduce the risk to safety.
- No practical, less intrusive alternative such as regular medicals, education, counseling, or some combination of these, would significantly reduce the risk to safety.[9]

E-Mail, Voice Mail...Video's Next

Another way that employers monitor the activities of their employees is to covertly access their electronic mail (e-mail) communications. E-mail is a paperless form of communication that can take place over a variety of networks, allowing messages to be sent from one computer to another (or to 5 or 500). Whether employers should be able to intercept employees' e-mail at the workplace has been debated at some length. Once again, employers have a right to see what their employees are doing and how they are spending their time on the job, but employees should be told this is happening and how it's happening.

One rationale is that employees should not be sending personal e-mail on company time, using company equipment. But the same argument holds true for the telephone—just because this equipment is provided by the company doesn't mean that employees' telephone lines should be bugged. While most employers don't condone this practice, they seem less reluctant to intercept e-mail communications. Could it be the ease with which it may be done without anyone knowing? Or is it simply that if the technology allows you to do it, it is too difficult to resist the temptation? It doesn't sound like a good idea to us, but again, if employers intend to monitor their employees' e-mail, then they should first tell their employees, allowing them to act accordingly.

Many people operate under the mistaken belief that e-mail, much like the mail they send through the post, is confidential and secure. In reality, the security of e-mail has been compared to the security of a postcard: both are open and accessible to being read by third parties. In *Protect Your Privacy*, William Stallings, a noted computer communications expert, asks: "When you write a personal letter to your doctor, lawyer, or lover, do you use a postcard? When you mail important documents to your accountant or business colleague, do you leave the envelope unsealed? Few people would answer yes to such questions....Yet millions of people use electronic mail for all kinds of messages and documents without giving a thought to privacy."[10]

The first step toward dispelling the myth of e-mail security is to make sure staff is informed about the realities of e-mail, including the employer's expectations of its use in the workplace. A written policy that lays out the rules that everyone must follow is a good idea, and employees should have input when the policy is being written.

Voice mail is an electronic version of the answering machine. A growing number of businesses are moving away from live bodies taking messages and toward voice messaging systems. However, the same problems encountered with e-mail systems arise—notably, the ease with which employees' voice-mail messages can be intercepted without their knowledge.

But quite apart from intentional interception, accidental access to voice mail also occurs through such things as computer problems, as one lawyer was quick to learn. Upon placing a call, she inadvertently tapped into someone else's voice-mail message, an extremely sensitive one about sex between two people having an illicit affair. The incident raised doubts in her mind about the confidentiality of the voice mail she received on her own system: "You think you've got this privacy, but you don't." The telephone company explained that a computer glitch was responsible for the errant message, and added that "people should be careful with any message they leave on any communication system." Consider yourself warned.

Intentional interception of personal voice-mail messages represents a considerable invasion of privacy. Michael Huffcut of Elmira, New York filed what may be the first invasion-of-privacy lawsuit for voice mail against his employer, McDonald's. Huffcut had worked at McDonald's as a supervisor for close to 20 years, when he had a brief affair with an assistant manager. During that time, they would leave what have been described as very personal love messages for each other on their voice-mail boxes. Huffcut had been told that he alone possessed the code to receive his voice messages; he alleges that his employer not only taped his messages but played them back to his wife. Huffcut confronted his employer about the incident and was fired several days later. The couple has allegedly experienced much anguish over this incident, although they have since reconciled, and Mrs. Huffcut has joined her husband as a plaintiff in a $2-million suit, claiming "severe emotional distress" as well as other injuries.

In the United States, the Electronic Communications Privacy Act offers protection for recorded electronic communications. While the law permits employers to monitor employees' telephone conversations for the purpose of ensuring that they are courteous and competent, listening to personal conversations has not been found permissible under a federal appeals court ruling.

Intentionally intercepting voice-mail messages at the workplace should be regarded as an invasion of privacy unless you work at a company where personal calls are prohibited. If a business must engage in this type of monitoring, we again recommend that staff and management together develop a policy governing its use. Give employees a chance to be treated fairly. Better still, don't listen in. And when video communications and their corresponding "video mail" become popular, don't "watch in."

Multimedia: Active Badge, Cruiser, and Rave

Multimedia networked communications permit various media to connect the workplace in a virtual sense: your boss need not be in your office to know what you're doing. He can see you via the camera in your office (connected to the network) and hear you via the microphone (also online). While these new "media spaces" permit closer contact among colleagues and aid collaboration, they can also be an unwelcome intrusion into one's work space, another high-tech tool for surveillance.

There are a variety of multimedia services starting with Olivetti's Active Badge, which when worn or carried tracks your location in a building and records when and where you were last observed. This can be a useful aid to find you (if you wish to be found), but other people may have access to the record of your movements. You have to be sure that the people who are in control of the system respect your privacy and have protections built in. Other, more sophisticated applications, such as Bellcore's Cruiser and Xerox EuroParc's Rave, offer services ranging from complete two-way video/audio connections lasting an indefinite time ("office sharing") to brief connections only a few seconds long ("glancing"); other connections may last as long as a conversation ("calling"). In examining the privacy implications of multimedia spaces, Andrew Clement finds that privacy is among the first issues people raise when they learn about these technologies. He comments that "ever-present microphones and cameras at close quarters carrying sensitive information about personal activities to remote and potentially unseen observers invite questions about possible abuse. This technical configuration is uncannily similar to that deployed by Big Brother in *Nineteen Eighty-Four*."[11]

Thus, it should come as no surprise that people have concerns regarding their ability to preserve their privacy in the midst of these media spaces, which, Professor Clement says, "provide the technical infrastructure for fine-grained, relentless, and unobtrusive employee surveillance unprecedented in its scope and reach." Granted, technical intent and actual practice may differ, but without privacy-protective features built in, intrusiveness may one day be the norm. To that end, a number of features are being built into the software to prevent interruption or intrusion, or to alert the individual that someone is "approaching"—in essence, to permit some element of control over one's accessibility. To prevent unwelcome intrusions, for example, electronic barriers may be erected; privacy "doors" may be closed or left slightly ajar.

Even with these modifications, a major concern of users is their ability to control how and to whom they expose themselves. Once again we return to the question of control and our overarching desire to preserve it. Fortunately, methods have been introduced to Cruiser, Rave, and similar applications that offer people choices about how much privacy they wish to have, thereby giving considerable control back to the individual.

Researchers Bellotti and Sellen have developed a set of design principles for "ubiquitous computing environments" revolving around the need for feedback and control.[12] They define control as "empowering people to stipulate what information they project and who can get hold of it," and feedback as "informing people when and what information about them is being captured and to whom the information is being made available." These principles are to be applied to four "classes of concern" that roughly depict the flow of information: capture (what information are they getting?), construction (what will happen to the information?), accessibility (who will have access to the information?), and purpose (how will the information be used?). Throughout the process, the need for "mutual awareness" and reciprocity ("If I can see you, you can see me") has been emphasized as an important design principle. Professor Clement has taken Bellotti and Sellen's principles a step further by recasting them in the language of data protection—Fair Information Practices—which revolves around the need for individual control and informational self-determination. Weaving the two together results in an optimum state of privacy protection for multimedia spaces. We recommend that developers of such models consider taking this approach.

Employee Records

Whatever your employer learns about you from any form of electronic surveillance or testing, or other sources of information, will probably be stored in your employee file. Go and take a look at it. Make sure the information is accurate and relevant to your work. If you are an employer, give your employees the right of access to their employment records; it will help you in the long run to have the most accurate information on which to base your decisions.

Several years ago, a study of Fortune 500 companies found that half of those surveyed had used employee medical records in making employment decisions. Of those, 20 percent had not informed the employee. A 1991 study by the Office of Technology Assessment of the U.S. Congress found that "almost a third of the employers that maintained employee medical records let their personnel departments read those records without notifying the employee."

With the growth of company-sponsored employee assistance programs, an enormous amount of sensitive personal information may come into the hands of your employer. Before participating in such a plan, make sure you know what information will be kept on file and what the terms of release are to your employer or to other third parties. If you are not comfortable with the terms, don't sign the release form (as difficult as that may be, since refusing may jeopardize your participation in a much-needed program). If you choose to sign it, do so with your eyes open, knowing that what you disclose during the course of the program may be revealed to your employer and other parties.

Concluding Thought

As an employee, you are entitled to a reasonable expectation of privacy in the workplace, particularly in the context of nonoccupational activities. Seek access to your employee file and check it for accuracy. If you think your work is being electronically monitored, talk to your employer and find out why. Do not assume that information contained in your e-mail, voice mail, or electronic files is confidential and secure. It is not. Act accordingly.

Endnotes

1. Information and Privacy Commissioner/Ontario, *Workplace Privacy: The Need for a Safety Net,* (Toronto: Information and Privacy Commissioner/Ontario, November 1993), p. 2.

2. Karen Nussbaum, "Workers Under Surveillance," *Computerworld,* Vol. 36, No. 1 (January 6, 1992), p. 21.

3. Robert Fulford, "Tolerating Electronic Sweatshops," *Globe and Mail,* December 14, 1994.

4. Andrew Clement,"Electronic Workplace Surveillance: Sweatshops and Fishbowls," *Canadian Journal of Information Science,* Vol. 17, No. 4 (December 1992), p. 25.

5. Bruce Feldthusen, quoted in John Ward, "Big Boss Snoops: Privacy Is Lost in Hi-Tech Workplace," *Toronto Sun*, July 6, 1994.

6. Information and Privacy Commissioner/Ontario, Foreword to *Workplace Privacy: A Consultation Paper*, (Toronto: Information and Privacy Commissioner/Ontario, June 1992), p. 2.

7. Privacy Commissioner of Canada, *Drug Testing and Privacy* (Ottawa: Privacy Commissioner of Canada, 1990), pp. 11, 12.

8. Max Yalden, quoted in a *Globe and Mail* editorial, "Drug Testing Rule Acceptable," August 17, 1994.

9. Privacy Commissioner of Canada, *Drug Testing*, p. 45.

10. William Stallings, *Protect Your Privacy: A Guide for PGP Users* (Englewood Cliffs, N.J.: Prentice-Hall, 1995), p. 1.

11. Andrew Clement, "Considering Privacy in the Development of Multi-Media Communications," *Computer Supported Cooperative Work*, Vol. 2 (1994), p. 70.

12. Victoria Bellotti and Abigail Sellen, "Design for Privacy in Ubiquitous Computing Environments," in *Proceedings of the European CSCW* (Milan: Kluwer, 1993), p. 80.

THE FUTURE...
WHAT'S IN IT
FOR US?

Technologies of Privacy, Technologies of Surveillance

An online civilization requires online anonymity, online identification, online authentication, online repudiation, online trustholders, online signatures, online privacy, and online access.

KEVIN KELLY
Wired Magazine

A great deal has been said about information technologies that threaten to diminish your privacy—technologies that chip away at your privacy, bit by bit, by electronically tracking your activities, transactions, and communications. Every time you use a credit card, make a telephone call, order something from a catalog, or subscribe to a magazine, you leave behind a data trail that can be picked up by these tracking technologies, which then link diverse pieces of information about you to form a digital picture of your personal preferences, your habits, your likes and dislikes.

But the consequences of these intrusive technologies do not just present themselves in the form of annoyances or intrusions from your forays into the marketplace. With the rise of new technologies like transponders and intelligent transportation systems (ITS), and developments on the information highway, it won't be long before everything is connected to everything else—electronically linked to portray a more comprehensive image of your digital persona. All this is predicated on one thing: identifier-based information—that is, personally identifiable information about you, containing your name or a unique identifying number. Without a personal identifier, information collected about your activities would pose no threat to your privacy, since it would remain anonymous and could not be linked to you. It would simply be information about an unknown individual.

Technologies of Privacy

Is it possible for new technologies to be designed in such a way that the default is set at zero-collection of personal information? Is it possible for technology to collect information from transactions anonymously without revealing your identity but ensuring the necessary authentication (proof that you are who you say you are)? Organizations understandably require the latter; otherwise they would be vulnerable to fraud. In the electronic marketplace, what is needed is the electronic equivalent of cash, which is both authentic and anonymous: when you pay with cash, the store is immediately assured of the validity of your payment (authentication) but does not possess the means to track the record of your purchase, since with a cash payment you do not divulge any identifying information. Cryptographers such as David Chaum, head of the Center for Mathematics and Computer Science in Amsterdam, say this system can be achieved electronically. Chaum has formed a company called DigiCash—short for digital cash—that promises to provide an electronic form of payment that is both anonymous and authentic.

Cryptography: Personal Encryption

Digital cash is only one use of encryption. Encryption techniques have traditionally been used for security purposes to protect the confidentiality of information and keep it secure from access by uninvited third parties. It may also be used to enhance communications privacy by protecting the identity of the parties communicating or transmitting information along a network.

Encryption, or encoding, is a mathematical process that disguises the content of the messages transmitted. Encryption provides us with a means by which to lock and unlock information transmitted along a network or stored in a database. To do this, the system must be able to conceal (encode or encrypt) information, and the intended recipient must be able to reveal (decode or decrypt) that information. The system must also be able to authenticate (verify) the identity or source of a transaction or communication.

Remember, as a child, when you had a secret code or language that only you and your best friend could understand? The purpose it served was to allow two people to communicate in some type of code (cipher) that was meaningful only to them, so that they, and no one else, could understand what was being said. Encryption is a similar process—it permits the sender of a message, typically known as "Alice," to lock or encode the content of a message in such a way that anyone else trying to intercept it would get only garbled text or "cipher text," as opposed to intelligible "plain text," or readable language. The intended receiver of the message, typically "Bob," would also have knowledge of the code used, so that he could unlock or decode it back into plain text, and be able to read it freely.

A simple example of encryption is the "Caesar" system, in which each letter in a plain text message is substituted with a letter three removed from it in the cipher text message. For example, "A" would appear as "D," "C" as "F," and "T" as "W." So if you wanted to tell someone "ACT NOW" you would send the cipher text message, "DFW QRZ." But things have gotten much more complicated since Caesar's day.

The area of encryption is very complex, building on mathematical computations known as algorithms. A rudimentary explanation of encryption will be provided here. Readers who wish to explore the subject in greater depth are referred to *Applied Cryptography,* an excellent text by Bruce Schneier, an expert in the field. In addition, David Banisar of EPIC has compiled the *1994 Cryptography and Privacy Sourcebook,* consisting of primary documents on U.S. encryption policy, the Clipper chip, digital telephony, and export controls. David Chaum's 1992 *Scientific American* article, "Achieving Electronic Privacy," also provides a good source for advanced reading on privacy and encryption.

The two main types of encryption are symmetric cryptosystems and public key cryptosystems. In *symmetric systems,* one common key (an extremely large number) is shared by both parties for encrypting and decrypting messages. Alice and Bob would possess the same key and use it to both encode and decode their electronic messages (hence, the symmetry). One problem with symmetric systems is that for you to be able to decrypt the message, the sender must tell you what the key is, and when that information is transmitted via a public network, it may be intercepted. Thus, the problem of key management has been identified as one of the drawbacks of symmetric cryptosystems.

A *public key system* of encryption is asymmetric, in that two different keys are involved: one public (widely distributed), one private (secret, known only to you). One would be used to encrypt a message, the other to decrypt it. What is encrypted with one key may be decrypted only with the corresponding key in the pair. One of the drawbacks of public key systems is that they tend to be slower than symmetric systems. It is possible, however, to combine the advantages of both systems in a "hybrid" cryptosystem, thereby yielding the greatest benefit for use in practical applications.

Whitfield Diffie and Martin Hellman invented the public key system of encryption in 1976. The Diffie-Hellman public key exchange has been called "the most revolutionary new concept in the field since the Renaissance." RSA, the most well-known public key system, was developed by Rivest, Shamir, and Adleman in 1978.

Steven Levy, author of *Hackers* and a columnist for *MacWorld,* applauds the benefits of a public key encryption system: "It enables people to communicate in complete secrecy with people they've never met....Even more remarkable, it makes possible a 'digital signature' assuring that an electronic message was generated by the person who claims responsibility for it. Together, these features allow us to create new forms of digital commerce with an unprecedented level of privacy."[1]

Under a public key system, you would publish your public key in a directory of public keys for subscribers to the system.

A secure message could be sent to you by anyone encrypting it with your public key, but only you, the holder of your private key, could decode the message—both parts are necessary to complete the process. So if Alice wanted to send Bob a confidential message, she would look up Bob's public key in the directory and use it as the encrypting key to transmit her message. Only Bob, the holder of the corresponding private key, could read the message sent to his public key. This process of using someone's public key to encode a confidential message is referred to as the encryption mode.

A public key may also be used as the decoding key, with the private key serving to encode the message. Since your private key is known only to you, when it is used to encrypt a message it is uniquely associated with you, much like a handwritten signature. So when a message is encoded with your private key, it serves as your "digital signature," to verify the identity of the sender and to ensure the integrity of the message. This form of encryption is referred to as the authentication mode, because it is used to verify the authenticity of the party sending the message. Here, the public key is used to decode a message which only the holder of the corresponding private key could have created. This feature can be used to create the digital equivalent of a handwritten signature, which serves to authenticate the transaction associated with it.

Digital Signatures and Blind Signatures

Although the digital signature provides an organization with the assurance that the person who signed the message being sent is in fact the person who sent it, David Chaum argues that one problem with such a system is that it offers no true privacy because the parties engaged in the transaction are identifiable and may ultimately be linked to their transactions. Chaum's "blind signature" technique, however, provides a solution to the problem by making anonymous one's identity, thus rendering it "blind."

Chaum states that transactions or communications using his system of blind signatures are "unconditionally untraceable," therefore providing an assurance of anonymity while preserving the authentication features of digital signatures. The beauty of such a system of anonymous signature transporting is that while your identity is untraceable (because it remains unknown), it can be made traceable at those times when it should be—when there is a legitimate need to trace your activities, for example, to ensure that you have reported your total income to the government and paid your fair share of taxes. Chaum designed the system in such a way that "transactions employing these techniques avoid the possibility of fraud, while maintaining the privacy of those who use them."

You don't need to worry about how to create a digital signature or what it would look like—it would automatically be produced for you. It could be the product of two large prime numbers (100 or more digits) that would be generated by a "smart card," a small credit card containing a microchip capable of carrying out the necessary computations. Though not impossible, public key systems are virtually unbreakable in practice. As Bruce Schneier notes in *Applied Cryptography*, "Good cryptosystems are designed to be unfeasible to break with the computating power that is expected to evolve many years in the future." Technologies of privacy such as public key encryption and blind signatures can be used to control the excesses of technologies used for surveillance.

An article in *The Economist* entitled "No Hiding Place: The Technologies That Make Life Easier Are Eroding People's Privacy" commented on the need for anonymous technologies where the guiding principle should be "to leave as much control as possible in the hands of individuals....Even if the anonymous technologies are more expensive and less convenient than the data-scooping alternatives, the price will be worth paying."[2] But anonymity need not necessarily cost more. As the price of fast computers with more powerful microchips goes down, so will the cost and speed of encrypted systems such as blind signatures. In 1994 Chaum's DigiCash launched the first electronic cash payment system over computer networks. Its news release announced: "Payment from any personal computer to any other workstation, over e-mail or Internet, has been demonstrated for the first time, using electronic cash technology....The possibilities are truly unlimited."

A viable form of electronic cash is therefore now available for payment over computer networks. This and other forms of encrypted, privacy-protective solutions are not far off. According to Kevin Kelly of *Wired*, "Efficient means of authentication and verification such as smart cards, tamper-proof networks, and microsized encryption chips are driving the cost of ciphers down to the consumer level. Encryption is now affordable for every man."

An example of a good system of public key encryption that is freely available is PGP, short for Pretty Good Privacy, developed by Phil Zimmermann. Zimmermann created a program that makes computer files and electronic mail almost "spy-proof." Then he gave it away to anyone for the asking. It appears that PGP has quickly found its way beyond North America to Europe, despite munitions export control laws that prevent the export of American encryption systems. The case against Zimmermann lodged by the U. S. federal government, spanning over 3 years, has finally ended: in early January 1996, he was informed that all charges would be dropped and the investigation closed. Justice at last! Zimmermann views the spread of PGP "as a symbol of people's determination to defend their right to privacy." And thanks to Phil Zimmermann, good encryption is available to everyone.

In *Applied Cryptography*, Bruce Schneier asks: "Does the average person really need this kind of security? I say yes. He may be planning a political campaign, discussing his taxes, or having an illicit affair....He may be living in a country that does not respect the rights of privacy of its citizens....Whatever his reasons, his data and communications are personal, private, and nobody's business but his own."[3] Preserving the privacy of our communications in the future may depend on such technologies as encryption and blind signatures. And as Kevin Kelly says, "Personal encryption may be as revolutionary as personal computers in transforming the web of communication."[4]

Anonymous Remailers

Another way to preserve your anonymity on the Internet is to channel your e-mail through "anonymous remailers"—a free service that strips the identifying header from your e-mail and then forwards it to the intended recipient. When you send a letter through regular mail, you have the option of maintaining anonymity: you don't have to put your return address on the envelope. On the Net, however, your e-mail address will automatically be sent unless you take steps to stop it, such as encrypting it or sending it through a remailer. Check out the "Internet Privacy Provider" for a range of anonymous services (http://www.anonymizer.com). Some people channel their mail through a series of remailers to further ensure that they remain anonymous; others first encrypt their e-mail address and then send it through a remailer for maximum screening.

But Where Will the *Will* Come From?

We believe that the choice of whether to use existing identifier-based technologies or privacy-protective anonymous ones will ultimately hinge not on cost but rather on the will to adopt such techniques—to relinquish the existing practice of compiling massive amounts of personal information. But who will lead the way? It is highly unlikely that either government or business will rush to embrace anonymous technologies. Most organizations want to collect more, not less, identifiable information, but privacy-protective anonymous technologies preclude collecting and storing identifiable personal information. While offering heightened security, they also offer uncompromising privacy: no more tracking of your activities and habits, since there is literally nothing to track.

Would there be any political will to pursue such technologies? We think it would have to come from you, the people, and your voices may have to be heard soon if the excesses of the technologies of surveillance are to be controlled.

Security Will Be Key

> Connectedness has become the Holy Grail of the 1990s….But in spite of the higher risks and higher stakes, little attention has been paid to the need for enhanced security….In spite of repeated examples of the vulnerability of almost all computer systems to invasion and manipulation, very few people recognize the magnitude of the damage that can be done, and even fewer have taken adequate steps to fix the problem. —Peter G. Neumann, *Issues in Science and Technology,* 1994

In the past, information security has been paid lip service but has usually been overshadowed by more pressing concerns. This is about to change. With personal communications and business dealings depending more and more on electronic networks, concern for the security of the transmitted information is beginning to grow. Two pertinent headlines appeared in the *Wall Street Journal* and the *New York Times* in early 1995: "Computer Experts See Hackers Gaining an Upper Hand in Fight over Security" and "Data Network Found Open to New Threat: Intruders Find New Route into Computers via Internet."

The ease with which those "in the know" can break into computer systems and gain access to your files is staggering, given the extensive use made of networked communications. In the years ahead, when the digital economy is global and is the main way of doing business, business may rely almost exclusively on networked communications. Personal communications via e-mail will also be used more frequently as more people discover the ease with which they can converse with friends and colleagues anywhere in the world. All of this may be compromised if secure methods of transmitting information and safeguarding personal files are not widely adopted. Without such protection, not only may the confidentiality of your information be jeopardized but documents may be destroyed, stolen, or worse, altered without you or the recipient ever knowing. Consider the implications for business, or for researchers exchanging data from recent experiments, if the very integrity of the information transmitted electronically is in question.

Fortunately, the solution to these concerns already exists: as noted earlier, encryption of information transmitted via networks or stored in computer databases will provide much-needed security and privacy protection. Most security experts say that true security on the Internet awaits the widespread adoption of encryption techniques for encoding data and authenticating messages. When questioned about the recent computer break-in and theft of his files, Tsutomu Shimomura, a senior fellow at the San Diego Supercomputer Center and a leading security expert, said, "Without improved methods of security such as encryption, it will just get worse."

And in a fully wired world, security will be a must. But let's not forget the growing world of wireless communications, which is poised for enormous growth in the next few years. But will wireless methods be secure? They can be—if security is built in. The developers of wireless packet-switched data networks such as Mobitex recognize the need for security and privacy, and have built it into their networks, not just with secure digital technology but with data encryption as well. "The combination of digital technology and packet data switching has produced a high degree of inherent security to safeguard the privacy of users' data. The additional use of protocols and unique radio modem designs makes it difficult to tap into Mobitex networks....Data encryption at the user application level provides the best protection of user data."[5] This is a welcome development. Encryption is among the most powerful forms of data protection available, and having it built into the system is extremely desirable.

Forms of security other than encryption should also be encouraged. These include protected passwords, tiered levels of entry, partitioned access according to sensitivity of files, rigorously enforced operating procedures, protocols, physical controls, and the use of firewalls. But they will not be enough. Peter Neumann, an expert on computer security, says that collective action will be needed at a variety of levels if security is to be taken seriously and our existing "head in the sand" mentality is to change. He feels that an information campaign is necessary to make both computer users and systems administrators alike "aware of how vulnerable their systems are to attack so that they will be motivated to employ defensive techniques. This must be a shared responsibility among vendors, customers, universities, and government organizations."[6]

In short, a heightened sense of urgency is needed among all groups to bring about improved systems and network security. Again, all that appears to be lacking is the *will* to take the necessary action.

A survey conducted in 1994 by Ernst and Young on information security tends to confirm the "head in the sand" view of the need to take action on data security.[7] Of the more than 1200 organizations that responded, representing a cross section of industries, 79 percent indicated that risks to information security had increased. Combine this with the fact that senior management does not tend to view security as a matter of serious concern, and you have the ingredients for a disaster. In the words of one survey respondent, "It is apparently going to take a major security breach before this organization gets its act together." That's just what it might take to give the issue the attention that is needed. Among those respondents who run their business systems on local area networks, 50 percent considered security unsatisfactory. This figure was even higher for organizations with more than 2500 employees: 55 percent reported that security was unsatisfactory for systems that were vital to their business operations.

What we may all require in the not-too-distant world of information highways and cyberspace is privacy-enhanced security. In a networked universe, technologies of privacy such as encryption may become a necessity, not a luxury. These technologies will restore some semblance of the past in a world that will otherwise be transformed by technologies of surveillance.

Technologies of Surveillance

The Clipper Chip

Developed by the U.S. National Security Agency (NSA), the Clipper chip is an encrypting microchip that, when installed into telephones or other communications media, scrambles the message to all but the intended parties. The U.S. government has proposed to introduce the Clipper chip into all communications systems in the nation. At first glance, it looks like a good idea: built-in protected communications. But there's a catch: Clipper has a "back door" that would allow government agencies, such as the FBI or NSA, to eavesdrop for purposes of national security or law enforcement. In *Applied Cryptography*, Bruce Schneier outlines the problem:

> Clipper is based on the Orwellian assumption that government has the right to listen to private communications. It promotes the power of the government over the power of the individual. This is not simply a little government proposal in some obscure area; it is a preemptive and unilateral attempt to usurp the powers that previously belonged to the people....Clipper does not protect privacy; it forces individuals to unconditionally trust that the government will respect their privacy.[8]

The proposal has generated intense opposition from both industry and the public. Eighty percent of those polled by Time/CNN in early 1994 opposed the idea of the Clipper chip. Computer Professionals for Social Responsibility organized an electronic petition seeking the withdrawal of the Clipper proposal and obtained almost 50,000 signatures in a month—among them, many of the world's most prominent computer security and cryptography experts.

Internet visionary and cofounder of the Electronic Frontier Foundation John Perry Barlow is not persuaded that the Clipper chip will aid law enforcement, but fears it will increase surveillance and diminish privacy in the process. Barlow points out that the Clipper chip is currently intended to be a voluntary standard, in which case, the "bad guys" would be unlikely to use it. "Even its most ardent proponents admit no intelligent criminal would trust communications to a key escrow device."[9] Wiretapping is not a primary tool for law enforcement; it is an investigative method of last resort. For example, in 1992, 919 wiretaps were authorized in the United

States; 607 people were convicted as a result of these wire-taps. The Electronic Privacy Information Center (EPIC), one of the strongest opponents of Clipper, points out that this number is a tiny fraction of all convictions, and stresses that the FBI has provided no evidence that any investigation has ever been jeopardized by the inability to perform a wiretap. So why introduce such an intrusive system of surveillance when the net return is expected to be so little?

Barlow writes of the Clipper chip's long-term implications for surveillance:

> In secret, they are making for us what may be the most important choice that has ever faced American democracy—that is, whether our descendants will lead their private lives with unprecedented mobility and safety from coercion, or whether every move they make, geographic, economic, or amorous, will be visible to anyone who possesses whatever may constitute "lawful authority.".…There is a lot the combined forces of government will be able to do to monitor all aspects of your behavior without getting a warrant.[10]

Whitfield Diffie, described by some as the elder statesman of cryptography, has actively opposed the Clipper chip, saying that it is impossible to trust secret mechanisms developed by an organization devoted mostly to spying. He cautions that in the days to come, maintaining our privacy will be an important ingredient of preserving our freedom: "Personal privacy certainly seems to me as important as ever, maybe more so. I'm firmly convinced that human freedom can't stand in the long run against improving communications technology that will utterly destroy the independence of the people."

In Canada, it would be foolish to believe that the Canadian counterpart to the NSA, the Communications Security Establishment (CSE), has not been keeping a watchful eye. In the words of the defense minister, "The CSE is Canada's cryptological organization that provides a vital security and communications function for the government of Canada and it is fully accountable to the minister of defense." Yet the public is not in a position to judge how accountable the CSE has been, because its activities are kept totally in the dark. The CSE has the ability to be extremely intrusive and has been accused of electronically spying on those holding legitimate but dissenting political views, such as Parti Quebeçois members René Levesque and Jacques Parizeau. The prime minister's assurances that no legitimate activities of Canadians are ever subject to CSE surveillance did not inspire great confidence, since no one was allowed to look closely at what the CSE was doing. The good news is that the federal privacy commissioner, Bruce Phillips, is trying—his office is conducting an audit of the CSE to determine whether it was in compliance with the Privacy Act. And in March 1995, the defense minister announced that he will be creating an independent agency to act as an external watch-dog over the CSE. Such an oversight mechanism will foster greater openness and accountability over the activities of this secretive agency.

The Digital Telephony Bill

Recently passed in the United States, the Digital Telephony bill, initiated by the FBI, permits law enforcement agencies to wiretap telephones and networked communications. Telephone companies are now required to make their new technologies "wiretap compatible." The bill, which may pave the way for the Clipper chip, sets a dangerous precedent. The Electronic Privacy Information Center, which lobbied long and hard against the bill, asked, "Where in the U.S. Constitution does it say that the federal government has the right to tap your phone?" As EPIC director Marc Rotenberg notes:

> To treat an investigative method of last resort as a design goal
> of first priority, as the Digital Telephony bill would do, is to
> stand wiretap law in this country on its head....Clipper and
> Digital Telephony pose grave threats to personal privacy. The
> premise of both proposals is that new communications tech-
> nologies should be designed to facilitate wire surveillance.
> This premise is contrary to the natural development of com-
> munications technology, which is to provide greater privacy.[11]

Government ID Cards

Another ominous threat to privacy comes in the form of a compulsory government ID card, to be used either as a multi-purpose national ID card or as a purpose-specific card to indicate, for example, landed-immigrant or social assistance status. Technology now allows for a digitized photograph or fingerprint to appear on the card, in addition to a unique identification number, all of which could be electronically maintained and linked with other pieces of personal information. Both the United States and Canada have recently explored the idea of introducing some form of identity card, as Australia did in 1985. Such a card could become another tool of the state to track the activities of its citizens, which is probably why so many people strongly oppose the idea; the so-called Australia Card was ultimately rejected in the face of strong public opposition. In his book about surveillance in Australia, Simon Davies writes that "thousands of people went to the streets, backing the government into a corner through the sheer and unprecedented force of public opinion."

On the face of it, tracking people within the borders of their own country with something like an internal passport seems innocent enough. Those in favor of ID cards point to their convenience, improved administrative efficiency, and how they aid in crime detection: the police could much more easily round up all the bad guys. Yet perhaps it is precisely the ease with which people could be pinpointed and "rounded up" that is troubling. We shouldn't forget Hitler's fond use of ID cards or, closer to home, how social security numbers were used to round up the Japanese during World War II. Imagine the potential for abuse in today's world of networked communications and data linkage—the ease with which targeted individuals could be monitored. Steve Moore, an economist at the U.S. Cato Institute think tank, regards national ID cards as "a fundamental invasion of privacy rights." People will no doubt continue to exclaim "we won't be numbers," as they did in Australia, and governments will no doubt continue to explore ways to quietly bring back identity cards.

Biometric Identification

What better combination to aid surveillance than to combine an ID card with irrefutable evidence of your identification? Biometric measures do just that by offering biological proof that you are indeed who you say you are. We are all familiar with the most common biometric measure, fingerprints. But there is now an expanding repertoire that includes retinal scans, palm prints, thumbprints, and DNA prints. These can all be stored in digitized form and therefore easily scanned by computers and transmitted along communications networks. Although this form of identification has historically been associated with policing, the use of biometric measures may well expand beyond this narrow realm– to identify welfare recipients, as one example.

The central problem with biometric measures is that once obtained, they are usually stored with the person's identity somewhere in a database, which can potentially be accessed by a number of third parties and used for a variety of purposes. This facilitates surveillance and makes it easier to track your movements and obtain information about you. Thus, the threat to privacy comes not from the positive identification that biometrics provides best, but from the ability of others to access this information in identifiable form (i.e., with your name on it) and link it with other personal information, facilitating the development of detailed personal profiles. However, this can happen only if the biometric information is kept in *identifiable* form. What if it was encrypted?

As discussed earlier, reliable forms of encryption prevent unauthorized third parties from accessing information they have no business accessing. When applied to biometric measures, they permit authentication of eligibility, without identification of the user. Take, for example, someone receiving welfare benefits. The government wants to eliminate fraud and ensure that only those eligible to receive these benefits actually do so. But if you *are* eligible, then you should get what you're entitled to. So what is needed is confirmation of the fact that person A (who we know is eligible for welfare benefits) is in fact person A and not someone impersonating him. *Biometric encryption* can do just that, without revealing the fact that person A is John Smith. So if person A uses these benefits to buy groceries (with food stamps, for example), he should be able to do so once his eligibility has been authenticated. You don't need to know that it's John Smith who went to the store to buy a head of lettuce, a loaf of bread, and some cheese. But you can be sure that someone else can't impersonate him and claim the same benefits—and fraud is thereby eliminated.

One enterprising company, Mytec Technologies Inc., has done just that. Mytec has developed the "bioscrypt," short for biometric encryption, which authenticates eligibility without divulging identity, thus preventing unauthorized access and use.

The bioscrypt bears no physical resemblance to the user's actual print. Nor does a copy of the print need to be kept on file. Since the bioscrypt was designed only to confirm an individual's identity, it can be used only for comparative purposes. Otherwise, it is meaningless—it cannot be used for any other purpose. Extension of this novel technology allows for the development of complete information systems using anonymous databases. George Tomko, president and CEO of Mytec, says that the bioscrypt system "precludes the need for a unique identifying number or the centralized storage of fingerprints. People can carry out their transactions privately in a 'blind manner' without the electronic tracing of a person's activities. Now transactions made through monetary systems such as credit or debit cards can be completely anonymous, thus ensuring total user privacy. With this technology, elimination of fraud is a by-product of protecting an individual's privacy."[12] Sound vaguely reminiscent? Refer back to David Chaum's blind signatures, which also provide maximum encrypted privacy. Systems such as these should receive our full support. They achieve the goal of fraud reduction (through positive confirmation of user eligibility) without giving away your identity or your privacy in the process.

Geographic Information Systems

Another type of surveillance may come in the form of a computerized database called a geographic information system (GIS). Typically, a GIS would display a map showing property lines, public areas, power transmission routes, natural resources, and so forth. It was intended for such purposes as helping municipalities select the best routes for public transportation or firefighters to get to various locations. When overlayed onto a grid of the streets of a particular city, the information contained in a GIS can pinpoint remarkably detailed information about the residents of a given city block. Considering how much of the digital information in databases today relates to economic and social interaction that has a geographic dimension, the possible applications of this extended use of GIS are quite disturbing. In a paper examining the privacy implications of GIS, Professor Michael Curry of the University of California in Los Angeles notes, "Typically, such a system includes, or can be used with, data about individuals or households. A marketer can create a profile of an individual, of that person's purchasing habits, automobile and home ownership, voting preference, religion, and so on, and then combine areal socioeconomic data with those individual data in order to create a profile of that person's 'lifestyle.'"

Global Positioning Satellites

Global positioning systems operate as another technology of surveillance in that they can pinpoint the location of objects such as cars or trucks, or people. These are satellite tracking systems that pinpoint and compile information about the movements of people or vehicles, the routes taken, the length and duration of trips, and so on. It doesn't take much tracking of your movements and activities to be able to predict a broad range of personal habits and behaviors. Combining this with information about you contained in other databases facilitates the development of a personal profile.

Intelligent Transportation Systems

Yet another technology of surveillance that will radically affect our privacy in the future is intelligent transportation systems, or ITS (formerly known as IVHS—intelligent vehicle highway systems). Coordinated by the U.S. Department of Transportation and the Transport Association of Canada, ITS will employ advanced information, communications, and sensor technologies to improve road safety and reduce traffic congestion. Who could argue with that? But in order for the system to perform some of these functions, a considerable amount of transaction-generated information will have to be collected, through a device such as an electronic tag or a transponder placed in your car to monitor its movements. Such tracking will inevitably lead to a recorded profile of your travel patterns—one more opportunity to track the movements of individuals as they go about their daily business. Once your travel is being monitored, it will be possible to infer a wide range of information, such as when people are or are not home and "where they work, spend leisure time, go to church, shop; what schools their children attend; where friends and associates live; whether they have been to see a doctor; and whether they attend political rallies."[13] Professor Philip Agre at the University of California, San Diego, an expert in this field, has studied ITS extensively. He says it "threatens to chill the freedom of association that is basic to a healthy democratic society."[14]

The available applications of ITS include satellite-based vehicle location, electronic identification and tracking devices, automated driving, and countless others that marry technology with vehicles and highways. ITS developments we can look forward to in the near future include pretrip and en route travel information, comprehensive traffic management, safety and pollution monitoring, personalized public transit through the use of smart cards, computerized route guidance and tracking, and automatic collision avoidance.

Yet these gains will be tempered by the potential for increased surveillance and diminished privacy. The possibilities grow more alarming if ITS information is linked with law enforcement, medical, insurance, lifestyle, or credit data. Linking travel data with other personal information will sharpen any profiles developed, making them that much more precise, and that much more valuable to governments, direct marketers, and many others.

Identifiable information about individuals collected through ITS will be available from numerous sources. One application of this technology, automatic vehicle identification (AVI), permits real-time tracking of the driver's travel through a transponder. There are certainly benefits to AVI, such as automatic toll collection along highways. Your car can be identified, the distance you travel logged, and an appropriate toll automatically debited from your account. But this convenience could add another set of eyes to those already watching.

It appears that these concerns are being noticed by others. The Legal Issues Committee of ITS America has developed a set of privacy principles that address such issues as ensuring the visibility and transparency of data collected, protecting the security and confidentiality of personal information, restricting the collection of information to only what is needed for ITS purposes, and providing consumers with a choice about the secondary uses of their information. "Persons who voluntarily participate in ITS programs...have a reasonable expectation that they will not be 'ambushed' by the information they are providing."[15]

Before we get as far as deciding about the secondary uses of this information, though, we first need to ask whether ITS programs can be packaged only in ways that, by necessity, must infringe on our privacy. As Professor Agre told us, the crucial issue is whether the systems developed capture individually identifiable information or provide the services anonymously. "Both approaches are technically feasible with current technology....All of the legitimate functionality of currently envisioned ITS systems can readily be implemented using temporary identifiers, digital cash, and other emerging technologies of privacy protection."[16] Once again, there *are* alternatives to the traditional identifier-based approach—ones that preserve your ability to move about in public spaces without concern that your movements will be systematically recorded; ones that do not require any identifiable information but nonetheless get the job done (e.g., electronic toll collection).

Which direction is more likely to be taken may again depend on your involvement. The privacy principles developed by ITS America don't give you a choice—they are based on the collection of identifiable information, followed by the regulation of where it goes. We think this is regrettable, and we are not alone. Professor Agre notes that the ITS principles make no mention of anonymity and, "are vague and offer little assurance that the information will not be abused. This vagueness is not simply a fault of the people who drafted them. It is effectively impossible to protect the privacy of data collected by ITS systems against subpoenas, claims by law enforcement, and commercial pressures toward secondary use. This is a compelling argument for the alternative approach based on anonymity." While the secondary uses of identifiable information do not appear to be among the main goals of the interest groups designing ITS systems, such uses will invariably develop, since they have clear commercial value.

An electronic toll system developed by David Chaum of DigiCash allows electronic devices to collect tolls automatically and, more important, anonymously, thereby protecting the identity of the driver. With his system of blind signatures and public key encryption, no transaction-generated information is yielded, eliminating the possibility of identifier-based movements being tracked. Chaum's electronic toll system has already been licensed to a Texas corporation, Amtech.

Privacy-protective systems are also being devised for cards that will automatically collect transit fares. The developer, Colin Plumb, states that whereas "it is possible for a card reader to keep detailed records of card usage without the card user's knowledge...the [card] reader can be designed so that it protects the card user's privacy by not keeping long-term records, which include tracking information."[17] Thus, anonymous technologies are not just wishful thinking; "privacy-clean" systems such as these are being implemented. The technology is there. All that is needed is the will to choose anonymous technologies over identifying ones.

Intrusive Telephones: Caller ID

Although many of these technological "advances" are still in the future for most of us, a package of services offered by telephone companies has the potential to threaten our communications privacy right now. One popular feature in telephone

Call Management Services (CMS) is Call Display, commonly referred to as Caller ID, which displays the caller's number on a small screen. The rationale behind Caller ID is that the receiver of the call should know who is calling, especially to avoid receiving harassing or obscene calls. But as Professor Rohan Samarajiva of Ohio State University, who specializes in telecommunications research, has noted, "The basic flaw in arguments in favor of Call Display is the assumption that more information will necessarily yield more control over the environment, specifically, over incoming calls."[18] There are better services offered through CMS to deal with disturbing calls. With Call Trace, for example, the phone company will automatically trace a harassing call and pass the information on to the police, at your request.

This all sounds reasonable on the face of it, but doesn't the caller have any privacy rights? If you have an unlisted number, or if you are returning a business call from your home in the evening, or if you just want some product information over the phone, you might not want to reveal your home number.

When it comes to nonpersonal calls, there may be numerous times when you might want to place a call anonymously, in order to obtain some information, such as the cost of a newly listed house for sale, or the price of a product or a new service you are considering (like a dating service). You just want some information. Why should companies be able to automatically capture your number, possibly for future use? The true benefits of Caller ID may lie more with its commercial uses than with its professed benefits to individuals. "The myth of Caller ID is that it will bring privacy and safety to telephone customers. What it will do instead is create new dangers. What happens to a child who has run away, or an abused wife, if they want to ring home?"[19] Women and children who do not want their whereabouts known but who may wish to call home will think twice before doing so.

In response to the concerns raised by individuals and consumer groups, telephone companies now offer a blocking feature, an option that permits you the caller to block the transmission of your telephone number, at no charge. When the

Canadian Radio-Television and Telecommunications Commission (CRTC) approved Caller ID in 1990, it allowed telephone companies to charge 75 cents for each blocked call and required that blocked calls be placed through a telephone operator. However, in the face of continuing protests from the public and consumer groups, the decision was finally reversed in 1992. In Canada, per-call blocking is now free, and as easy as pressing a few extra numbers (*67) before placing a call. The same is true in the United States.

Per-line blocking means that you can block your number from all the calls made from your line. But this choice is not yours to make in Canada because per-line blocking is offered only on a very limited basis, to such places as distress centers and women's shelters. With the recent introduction of Name Display, which displays your name as well as your telephone number, this limitation should be reconsidered. The telephone version of negative consent, or opting out, is the per-call blocking feature; per-line blocking corresponds to positive consent, or opting in. You should be able to determine for yourself whether and to what extent you are willing to identify yourself to the person at the other end of the line.

In the United States, a great deal of controversy was generated over a Federal Communications Commission (FCC) ruling. The FCC has jurisdiction over interstate communications, whereas individual states have jurisdiction over matters involving communications within the state. In 1994, the FCC ruled that free per-call (not per-line) blocking would be the standard for interstate calls. The ruling has caused considerable controversy, because many states already have in place the stronger privacy standard of per-line blocking, and the FCC decision would have the effect of preempting state rules. Forty-eight parties, including consumer groups and privacy advocates, petitioned the FCC to reconsider its decision. The California Public Utility Commission launched a court challenge to block the FCC decision, while others prepared to file lawsuits against the FCC if it adopted the proposed order. The chairman of the New York Public Service Commission, Peter Bradford, warned of the confusion and uncertainty the FCC order was bound to create: "Protracted litigation over the FCC decision is certain and may impede the introduction of inter-state Call ID services....Customer confusion and disappoint-ment with limitations on privacy options will spawn a host of complaints....[The FCC's] proposal is likely to damage the prospects for Caller ID and it is certain to damage federal-state relations in the communications area at a time when much depends on our mutual trust and cooperation."

In his petition for reconsideration, Professor Samarajiva noted that whereas the FCC had not held any public hearings before issuing its decision, 46 states had held hearings on Caller ID before reaching their decisions, well before the FCC's ruling. He further noted that the more information that became available on Caller ID, the more state utility commis-sions were requiring per-line—as well as per-call—blocking to be offered.[20]

The good news is that the FCC listened to these objections and reconsidered its proposal to only allow per-call blocking. In its May 4, 1995 ruling, the commission agreed to permit per-line blocking to remain in effect in the over 40 states that had already adopted the higher standard of privacy protection. This ruling came into effect December 1, 1995. Under the order, people with per-line blocking (which automatically blocks all calls made through that line) may *unblock* their number by pressing *82 if they wish to have it displayed to a Caller ID device. In addition, the FCC ruled that the name associated with a blocked line may not be revealed by carriers and that blocked numbers should be blocked from automatic call returns. This ruling comes as a major success for privacy advocates and the public alike.

ADADs

Not a form of surveillance but an intrusion on privacy nonethe-less are those annoying calls placed to your home by automatic dialing and answering devices known as ADADs. The CRTC received more complaints about ADADs than anything else. Consequently, to its credit, the CRTC banned the use of

ADADs for commercial solicitation in 1994, after attempts to regulate its use had failed. The rules that had been set down for businesses using ADADs had simply not been followed—an example of failed self-regulation. Little respect was being shown for consumers and little concern for intrusions into their privacy. When the CRTC pulled the plug, the message was clear: businesses employing intrusive communications techniques that failed to respect the privacy of those to whom they were marketing their products or services would fail.

In the United States, telecommunications are regulated at both the state and the federal level. ADADs have been banned only in some states, such as Maryland. On a positive note, however, a number of states give consumers the option of per-call or per-line blocking (which will now remain intact, unaffected by the latest FCC ruling). In New York State, for example, the default option is per-call blocking, with the ability to upgrade to per-line blocking; several states offer per-line blocking free of charge.

Telecom Privacy Principles

A number of principles have been developed to protect your privacy in the area of telecommunications. They reinforce your right to choose—to exert control over your personal information. They place an obligation on suppliers of services to make their customers aware of the privacy implications of new telecommunications technologies and products. They attempt to restore, at no additional charge, any privacy that is lost or diminished by new services. They restrict the use and disclosure of transactional data arising out of calls made. They require that a customer's informed consent be obtained for any secondary uses of those data. In short, they try to create a minimal threshold for privacy for all of us.

The following are four sets of telecommunications privacy principles: two from government, one from academia, and one from an organization committed to protecting privacy. Each is different, yet note the distinct similarities.

**New York State Public Service Commission
Statement of Policy on Privacy in
Telecommunications, 1991**

Principle No. 1 (Consideration of Privacy Effects)
Privacy should be recognized explicitly as an issue to be considered in introducing new telecommunications services.

Principle No. 2 (Importance of Open Network)   The interest in an open network should be recognized in evaluating alternative means for protecting privacy.

Principle No. 3 (Customer Education)   Companies should educate their customers as to the implications for privacy of the services they offer.

Principle No. 4 (Various Levels of Privacy)   People should be permitted to choose among various degrees of privacy protection, with respect to both the outflow of information about themselves and the receipt of incoming intrusions.

Principle No. 5 (Maintaining Current Privacy Expectations)
A telephone company offering a new service that compromises current privacy expectations would be obligated to offer a means of restoring the lost degree of privacy unless it showed good cause for not doing so.

Principle No. 6 (Pricing of Privacy Features)   Considerations of cost, public policy, economics, and technology all bear on the pricing of privacy features, which must be determined case by case.

Principle No. 7 (Customer Information)   Unless a subscriber grants informed consent, subscriber-specific information generated by the subscriber's use of a telecommunications service should be used only in connection with rendering or billing for that service or for other goods or services requested by the subscriber.

Principle No. 8 (Changing Expectations)   Privacy expectations may change over time, requiring, in some instances, changes in telecommunications services. At the same time, changes in telecommunications technology services and markets may lead to changes in customers' privacy expectations.

Department of Communications, Canada Telecommunications Privacy Principles, 1992

1. Canadians value their privacy. Personal privacy considerations must be addressed explicitly in the provision, use, and regulation of telecommunications services.

2. Canadians need to know the implications of the use of telecommunications services for their personal privacy. All providers of telecommunications services and government have a responsibility to communicate this information in an understandable and accessible form.

3. When telecommunications services that compromise personal privacy are introduced, appropriate measures must be taken to maintain the consumers' privacy at no extra cost unless there are compelling reasons for not doing so.

4. It is fundamental to privacy that there be limits to the collection, use, and disclosure of personal information obtained by service providers and generated by telecommunications networks. Except where clearly in the public interest, or as authorized by law, such information should be collected, used, and disclosed only with the express and informed consent of the persons involved.

5. Fundamental to privacy is the right to be left alone. A balance should exist between the legitimate use of unsolicited telecommunications and their potential for intrusion into personal privacy. All parties have a responsibility to establish ground rules and methods of redress so that Canadians are able to protect themselves from unwanted and intrusive telecommunications.

6. Privacy expectations of Canadians may change over time. Methods of protecting telecommunications privacy must be reviewed from time to time to meet these changing expectations and to respond to changing technologies and services.

Minimal Standards to Guarantee Communications Privacy, 1992
Professor Gary T. Marx, M.I.T.

1. No listening, viewing, or recording of communications without all parties' consent.

2. Fair warning so that if devices such as automatic number identification systems or speaker phones are in use, the other party is informed before the communication begins.

3. Joint ownership of transactional data so that all parties to a data-creating transaction must agree to any subsequent use of the data and must share in any gains from its sale.

4. Restoration—those technologically altering the privacy status quo should bear the cost of restoring it.

5. A safety net or equity principle guaranteeing a minimum threshold of privacy available to all, regardless of what technology is capable of doing. There should be limits on the extent to which privacy is treated as a commodity available only to those who can afford it.

6. Consistency so that broad ideals, rather than the specific characteristics of a technology, determine privacy protection. Thus, even though it is technically easy to listen in on personal radio transmissions over cordless phones, the same principle is being violated as if a corded phone conversation were to be overheard.

7. Redress—those subject to privacy invasions need adequate mechanisms for discovering violations and receiving compensation for them.

Computer Professionals for Social Responsibility Telecommunications Privacy Guidelines, 1993

1. The confidentiality of telecommunications should be protected.

2. Privacy considerations must be recognized explicitly in the provision, use, and regulation of telecommunications services.

3. The collection of personal data for telecommunication services should be limited to the extent necessary to provide the service.

4. Service providers should not disclose information without the explicit consent of service users. Service providers should be required to make known their data collection practices to service users.

5. Users should not be required to pay for routine privacy protection. Additional costs for privacy should be imposed only for extraordinary protection.

6. Service providers should be encouraged to explore technical means to protect privacy.

7. Appropriate security policies should be developed to protect network communications.

8. A mechanism should be established to ensure the observance of these principles.

A Time for Innovation

What is required is fresh, innovative thinking. Just because something is done a certain way now does not mean that it can't be changed to include privacy-protective options, thereby allowing consumers to make a choice. Take for example the way telephone companies issue our telephone statements: long-distance calls are fully itemized, containing dates, times, and locations of called numbers, as well as the complete telephone numbers called. In Europe, either detailed billing information is not available or, where it is available, the last four digits are not disclosed. NTT in Japan offers a range of privacy options for customers: customers may choose to receive complete details of calls, partial details, or no details at all. "Telephone systems can be designed to 'forget' the last few digits of a telephone number after placing a call, in order to protect privacy in personal billing statements. Electronic mail systems can be developed that provide ephemeral messages for personal use, a sort of electronic disappearing ink."[21] Services can also be billed in other ways—metered use is only one. Services could be billed on a bulk basis by access level, tiered to the level of service desired. For example, you might get to make 10 calls for $2, 20 for $3, and so on.

The point is that if we explore alternative ways of doing things, we will find privacy-protective options. We just have to look for them.

Concluding Thought

> There is a choice to be made between technologies of surveillance and technologies of privacy. One promises to collect vast amounts of personal information and track your movements and activities. The other promises anonymity, security, and the protection of your privacy. Both will get the job done. Both can be implemented. Which would you prefer? The choice may be yours to make only if you act now.

Endnotes

1. Steven Levy, "Prophet of Privacy," *Wired Magazine* (November 1994), p. 128.
2. "No Hiding Place: The Technologies That Make Life Easier Are Eroding People's Privacy," *The Economist* (August 1993), p. 16.
3. Bruce Schneier, *Applied Cryptography* (New York: John Wiley & Sons, 1994), pp. xv–xvi.
4. Kevin Kelly, "Cypherpunks, E-Money," *Whole Earth Review* (Summer 1993), p. 40.
5. "The Inherent Security of Data over Mobitex Wireless Packet Data Networks," A RAM Mobile Data White Paper (August 1994), pp. 1, 6.
6. Peter G. Neumann, "Computer Insecurity," *Issues in Science and Technology* (Fall 1994), p. 50.
7. Ernst and Young, *2nd Annual Information Security Survey: Trends, Concerns and Practices,* (Toronto: Ernst and Young, 1994).
8. Schneier, *Applied Cryptography,* p. xvi.

9. John Perry Barlow, "A Plain Text on Crypto Policy," *Communications of the ACM*, Vol. 36, No. 11 (November 1993), p. 21.

10. Barlow, "Plain Text," pp. 24–25.

11. Marc Rotenberg, "Wiretapping Bill: Costly and Intrusive," *Insight*, October 24, 1994, pp. 20, 21.

12. George J. Tomko, *Mytec Technologies Annual Report*, 1994. p.4

13. The Privacy Bulletin, in Sheri Alpert, "Privacy on Intelligent Highways: Finding the Right of Way," *The Santa Clara Computer and Technology Law Journal*, Vol. 11, No. 1 (March 1995), p. 97.

14. Philip E. Agre, personal communication, January 4, 1996.

15. IVHS America Legal Issues Committee, *Strawman Privacy Principles*. 1994, pp. 2–3.

16. Agre, personal communication.

17. Colin Plumb, "Protocol for Fare Collection Using a Contactless Memory Card," unpublished paper, Boulder Software Engineering, January 16 1995, p. 2.

18. Rohan Samarajiva, "Privacy in Electronic Public Space: Emerging Issues," *Canadian Journal of Communications*, Vol. 19 (1994), p. 94.

19. Simon Davies, *Big Brother: Australia's Growing Web of Surveillance* (Sydney: Simon & Schuster, 1992), p. 120.

20. Samarajiva, "Privacy in Electronic Public Space," p. 94.

21. Industry Canada, *Privacy and the Canadian Information Highway* (Ottawa: Industry Canada, October 1994), p.17.

Why Business Should Listen: Privacy Makes Good Sense

Giving the consumers [a] choice as to whether or not they want to participate in the marketing process not only makes good business sense but also meets the concerns of consumers head on.

JONAH GITLITZ
President, Direct Marketing Association

Surely You Jest?

You know by now that we've been leading up to this message throughout the entire book: privacy makes for good business. We realize that it may not be an obvious conclusion. Privacy protection has historically been viewed as an impediment to private enterprise. But the opposite may be the case. After all, extending privacy laws into the private sector did not cause an economic crisis in Quebec, nor did it bring the business community "to its knees," as was feared by some. Building privacy into your business practices from the start may actually enhance your business. Treating your customers with respect and recognizing their right to privacy will not only improve customer service but may also create a loyal following, which in turn will boost the bottom line.

The 1994 annual conference of Privacy Laws and Business had as its theme "Integrating Data Protection Law into Good Business Practice." Privacy, or data protection as it is called in Europe, was advanced as being good for business when integrated into day-to-day business practices. Unlike in North

America, data protection laws apply to the private sector in England and many European countries; evidently, commercial enterprise has not ground to a halt as a result of such laws.

Self-Regulating Voluntary Codes

Signs of privacy in the business community are also beginning to appear in North America. Businesses are paying more attention to the need for privacy in their day-to-day practices. Evidence is found in the growing number of voluntary industry codes of conduct for privacy. A wide range of sectors, from banking and insurance to direct marketing and telecommunications, have written their own privacy codes in an effort to fend off legislation and nurture a much-needed degree of confidence among their customers. For the most part, these industry codes have been modeled on the OECD's Code of Fair Information Practices, building in basic protections regarding limited collection, notification of intended uses, consent for secondary uses, and the right of access to one's file and correction of errors. Industry codes have the advantage of being tailor-made to the particular circumstances of one sector, allowing for greater flexibility in applying information practices. It is also more likely that sector-specific protections will suit the needs of the customers as well as the particular regulatory environment in which the industry must operate.

In the United States, such industry associations as the Direct Marketing Association and the Information Industry Association of America, to name but two, have produced their own privacy codes. In addition, a number of businesses such as American Express, Equifax, IBM, and Dun & Bradstreet have written their own company privacy codes. Likewise, a number of Canadian industry associations—including the Stentor Telecom Alliance, the Canadian Bankers Association, the Insurance Bureau of Canada, and the Canadian Direct Marketing Association—have developed codes for their member businesses. In addition, a number of companies have attempted to address the question of privacy in the services they offer. One example is a booklet called *Privacy and Your Telephone Service: A Guide for Bell Canada Customers*, which starts off by saying that "Canadians have come to expect that they have a basic right to live their lives in privacy."

Among the most important considerations for businesses in protecting their customers' privacy is a clear understanding and separation of the primary and secondary uses of the personal information they collect. An easily understandable "opt-out clause" must be offered to customers, allowing them to decide whether they wish to have their information used for any other (secondary) purposes. In a talk to the Privacy Laws and Business Conference, Professor Joel Reidenberg provided two examples that illustrate the difference between good and bad opt-out provisions. An example of a vague all-or-nothing opt-out is, "From time to time, companies ask to send their catalogs...to our customers...we allow it." You let them do this by either agreeing or not agreeing. Contrast this with the specific opt-out clause offered by American Express: "We develop mailing lists based on information you provide to us in surveys and information derived from how you use the card which may indicate shopping preferences and lifestyle as well as information available from public sources." This is accompanied by several options for customers to select from. (Amex was forced to provide notification to its customers. The New York attorney general reached a landmark agreement with the company that credit card holders should not have their spending patterns analyzed for solicitation or marketing purposes without their knowledge.)

Added choice ultimately benefits both customer and company, because it might be the case that you wouldn't mind having your information passed on for certain uses but definitely not for others. An all-or-nothing opt-out clause does not capture this sentiment. When one company moved from a yes/no opt-out clause to a multiple-selection one, it was pleasantly surprised. A number of customers who had opted out completely in the past now chose to partially opt in. The customers' major objection was to having their information passed on to telemarketers and to external third parties; the majority did not mind receiving commercial solicitations from the primary company along with their monthly bill. This points to the success of tailoring your program to meet the needs of your customers.

Voluntary privacy codes are believed to be less effective than ones entrenched in law, mainly because of the lack of an adequate enforcement mechanism. "There is no need for voluntary codes to be any less stringent than those enforced by law, but it is this very matter of enforceability that is giving consumer advocates grounds for concern...[voluntary codes] are considered by most privacy experts as inadequate to cope with the privacy threats of the 1990s."[1] In addition, consumer advocates remind us that voluntary codes have little, if any, consumer input, tend to be poorly monitored and poorly communicated, and leave consumers with little recourse if their complaints are not resolved. In short, one must rely on the good faith of the company, which at times may be lacking.

The need for privacy protection in the absence of privacy laws for the private sector has led the Canadian Standards Association (CSA) to develop a generic privacy code (CSA Model Code for the Protection of Personal Information), containing the CSA's stamp of approval, which private-sector organizations could use as a model. The CSA Model Code was finalized and unanimously passed on September 22, 1995. The project team consisted of leading corporations and businesses, representatives of the federal government, privacy advocates and consumer groups. What is novel about the CSA's approach is that, although the code is voluntary, an attempt has been made to build in an oversight mechanism to address the historic lack of enforcement of voluntary codes. The watchdog component of the code could come through some form of auditing and certification conducted by a respected standards body like the CSA. (The CSA already performs this function in other areas.) One must heed the caution, however, that the CSA code would need to be adopted broadly, by both companies and industry associations alike, to be truly effective.

The CSA privacy code, like most, is modeled on the OECD guidelines, except that it strengthens two components: "consent," by having it stand alone as a completely separate principle, and "challenging compliance," which strengthens a person's right to challenge an organization's compliance with any of the principles, not simply refusals of access or the accuracy of the collected data. As well, accountability was considered to be so fundamental that it was placed first in the list of 10 principles.

CSA Model Code for the Protection of Personal Information

1. *Accountability.* An organization is responsible for personal information under its control and shall designate a person who is accountable for the organization's compliance with the following principles.

2. *Identifying purposes.* The purposes for which personal information is collected shall be identified by the organization at or before the time the information is collected.

3. *Consent.* The knowledge and consent of the individual are required for the collection, use, or disclosure of personal information except where inappropriate.

4. *Limiting collection.* The collection of personal information shall be limited to that which is necessary for the purposes identified by the organization. Information shall be collected by fair and lawful means.

5. *Limiting use, disclosure, and retention.* Personal information shall not be used or disclosed for purposes other than those for which it was collected except with the consent of the individual or as required by law. Personal information shall be retained only as long as necessary for the fulfillment of those purposes.

6. *Accuracy.* Personal information shall be as accurate, complete, and up-to-date as is necessary for the purposes for which it is to be used.

7. *Safeguards.* Personal information shall be protected by security safeguards appropriate to the sensitivity of the information.

8. *Openness.* An organization shall make readily available to individuals specific information about its policies and practices relating to its handling of personal information.

9. *Individual access.*   Upon request, an individual shall be informed of the existence, use, and disclosure of personal information about the individual and shall be given access to that information. An individual shall be able to challenge the accuracy and completeness of the information and have it amended as appropriate.

10. *Challenging compliance.*   An individual shall be able to challenge compliance with the above principles with the person who is accountable within the organization.

Two other developments lend support to the view that the business community needs to take privacy protection seriously. Two new publications appeared in 1994. The first American magazine devoted to privacy and business, *Privacy and American Business*, introduces readers to timely surveys, analyses, and developments in the area of privacy. Described as "the only publication that is both business-friendly and privacy-sensitive," it is edited by privacy veteran Alan Westin. It also offers businesses a new information service: "Now, you can get up-to-date, authoritative, and balanced information resources on the key privacy issues affecting your company and industry."

The second publication is a thought-provoking report produced by the information and privacy commissioner of Ontario called *Privacy Protection Makes Good Business Sense*. Taking a common-sense approach, this report offers a number of privacy practices that business would be wise to consider. The report points out that the changing relationship between customers and businesses, from face-to-face encounters to electronic transactions, underscores the need for business to review its practices. Diminished personal contact with customers has transformed the way business uses customers' personal information. Instead of decisions being based on exchanges with customers with whom one interacts, decisions are increasingly based on information about customers drawn from various databases.

Information technology and the global business environment have radically altered the way individuals relate and interact with organizations....Decisions are based on a comprehensive "data image" developed by drawing together and analyzing information about an individual from diverse sources....Consumers feel vulnerable in the face of invasive and unrestricted information practices. Privacy is seen as one of the key social values being threatened by these practices.[2]

The report goes on to emphasize that some business needs legitimately require the collection of personal information. But the two goals of needing information for legitimate business purposes and privacy protection need not be mutually exclusive. Instead of competing against each other, the two can join forces if privacy-protective practices are built into one's business. In these times of fiercely competitive markets, if protecting consumer privacy is viewed as a component of good business practice, then privacy need not be treated as an adversary—it can be made an ally. When a company designs its products and services with privacy in mind, it also enhances the security of its information holdings, which in turn enhances customer confidence. That trust has considerable commercial value.

An additional benefit for business in having privacy-friendly practices is the greater accuracy of the resulting information. As the Information Technology Association puts it, "In the information economy, the quality and integrity of information is of paramount importance....[W]ithout accurate information about their customers, businesses are unable to effectively focus their efforts, time, or resources. This is costly and inefficient. The adoption of privacy-protection practices can assist businesses to concentrate their resources and to improve the quality of their customer service."[3]

In addition, involving customers in making choices about their preferences can become an indispensable aid to marketing departments, which must rely on accurate customer information for their targeting efforts. Why waste time and resources marketing products to people who have no interest in them? What's worse is that in the process you might antagonize them, making customers avoid your product or service in the future.

And in these days of fierce competition, enhanced customer service is no longer just a courtesy; it's a necessity. Those businesses offering privacy-friendly services to their customers will gain a competitive advantage over businesses that are less progressive. As indicated again and again in the polls, consumers want their privacy respected and they want to be able to make choices. Offer them the ability to choose and treat them with the respect they deserve, and your business will be much better positioned to do business in the twenty-first century. And if you do that, maybe your company will make it onto the Privacy Register, a list of companies proposed by Professor Colin Bennett that respect their customers' privacy and practice Fair Information Practices. In the future, consumers may check to see if your company is on this register before doing business with you. Just as there are now lists of companies that follow environmentally sound practices for those wishing to do business or invest, we predict that lists of privacy-protective companies will also emerge.

One thing is clear. Businesses can no longer take their customers for granted. The consumer of today has great expectations, and if you fail to meet them, the customer will move on to companies that can. When you treat consumers as partners and valued stakeholders, however, chances are that you will be able to keep their business. One credit-reporting agency's efforts to address privacy concerns came in the form of a publication for customers called *The 1993 Consumer Information and Privacy Report: The Equifax Perspective*. This report contains Equifax's updated Fair Information Practices—updated because the company recognized the importance of providing information to consumers and "the need for a continuing balance between the legitimate information needs of our economic system and the privacy interests of our citizens."

Quebec: A Privacy Success Story

Quebec is the first jurisdiction in North America to enact legislation that extends the right of privacy from the public sector to the private sector—the business community. Commonly referred to as Bill 68, the Act Respecting the Protection of Personal Information in the Private Sector came into force in 1994 and affects more than 800,000 businesses and private organizations, large and small. The Commission d'Access à l'Information, (CAI) is the oversight agency for privacy protection in Quebec and has overseen the public-sector privacy law—the Act Respecting the Access to Documents Held by Public Bodies and the Protection of Personal Information—since 1982.

Commission president Paul-André Comeau reported at a privacy conference in 1995 that commercial enterprises had been very cooperative in implementing the new legislation. He added, "There has been no catastrophe in Quebec. It's business as usual. The implementation of this important piece of legislation is running smoothly."

Comeau pointed out that the two privacy laws in Quebec, applicable to the public and private sectors, take precedence over all other Quebec statutes, laws, or municipal bylaws: "There are, in the body of Quebec laws, only a few provisions to which the legislator has given precedence, to stress their importance and to indicate that their underlying principles must not be violated without due consideration. The consequences of according precedence are substantial, for in a way, it binds the legislator for the future."*

Because of the pragmatic approach taken to Bill 68, multinational corporations such as American Express, banks, and credit bureaus such as Equifax quickly developed measures to comply with the legislation. What is of even greater benefit is that these companies have offices outside of Quebec, and there has already been a spillover effect of the new privacy practices. For example, the consent forms that were designed to meet the requirement that an individual's consent be free and informed have already been adopted by some businesses in their transactions with their customers and members outside the province. Perhaps companies such as American Express will extend these same practices to the United States. After all, it makes good business sense.

---

*Paul-André Comeau, "Understanding the Quebec Privacy Legislation and Discovering How It Will Impact Your Organization," paper presented at the conference Protecting Privacy in the Information Age, October 17–18, Toronto, Canada.

Bill 68 does not prevent businesses from exchanging mailing lists, and therefore does not threaten the direct-marketing industry. Yet certain parts of the act are aimed specifically at direct marketers. Although the law authorizes the release of nominative lists (those containing names, addresses, and telephone numbers), organizations intending to use information for secondary purposes must meet several requirements that compel them to act responsibly and openly declare the intended uses of the information.

Clear and understandable opt-out provisions are now required by law—all organizations must provide individuals with the opportunity to express their views about any secondary uses of their information. A person also has the right to have his or her information removed from lists. The CAI has made model consent forms available to all enterprises and has developed template opt-out clauses that can be adapted by businesses. (Under the law, opt-out provisions, or negative consent, may be used only for nominative mailing lists. For all other purposes, positive consent is required for collecting personal information.)

Any business wishing to use or disclose a nominative mailing list may do so only in accordance with a contract that stipulates that the information will be used only for legitimate commercial or philanthropic purposes, that an opportunity for individuals on the list to opt out has been provided up front, and that the disclosure or "communication" of the information contained on a nominative list does not infringe upon the privacy of the persons concerned. In addition, anyone wishing to have her or his personal information deleted from a list may request that at any time; organizations that receive such requests must abide by them.

The law has also introduced rules for "personal information agents," consisting primarily of credit bureaus. These agents must be registered with the CAI and must make their activities known to the public by periodically publishing a notice in local newspapers. Bill 68 contains stiff penalties for noncompliance: fines up to $20,000 may be imposed.

Many of the large law firms in Quebec have produced brochures and information pamphlets about the new legislation. The CAI has been conducting extensive training sessions, holding workshops, and speaking to organizations covered by the law. In the 10 months after the bill was passed, requests for information increased from 500 a week to 1700 a week.

One example of a large corporation that had to meet the requirements of the new law is Reader's Digest. Barbara Robins, legal counsel for Reader's Digest, spoke about the company's recent experience of "molding their business practices" to comply with Bill 68. While acknowledging that the transition was not a "seamless" one, she indicated that since the provisions relating to direct marketing were similar to the CDMA's voluntary privacy code, the new requirements were essentially "refinements of self-regulated practices."

The credit-reporting agency Equifax says that the number of customers requesting access to its credit files has doubled since 1993, presumably as a result of people learning about the new law. The company also introduced some new services, such as improved processing time, same-day to 7-day correction of errors, and notification of errors to companies that had received a credit report within the previous 6 months. Although some new costs were incurred as a result of complying with the new law, Equifax vice president Michel Globensky says that enhanced customer satisfaction has made the investment worthwhile.

In the first 6 months of Bill 68 being in operation, the CAI received 57 complaints of breaches. These complaints fell into three broad categories. The first included complaints about the absence of consent regarding the indirect collection of information from third parties. These complaints generally involved life insurance companies, which often required applicants to give blanket consent to the widespread collection of their information from third parties. Under the new law, insurance companies must limit the consent provisions to information that is truly required.

The second type of complaint involved employers' widespread access to employees' personal information, and how much of that information was legitimately required. For example, although an employer may need to know that an employee's work will be affected by a medical condition, the employer does not need to know what the medical condition is. All that is required is a finding by the employee's physician indicating that a medical condition exists and how it will affect the employee's work performance. Employers do not need detailed medical information.

The third major complaint involved direct marketing. Entire mailing lists containing names and addresses used to be handed over to third parties without the consent of the individuals listed. Bill 68 changed that. Since the law permits some limited forms of indirect collection for marketing purposes, individuals must be able to indicate that they do not wish to have their information passed on to third parties for secondary uses.

The CAI said it has received a great deal of cooperation from the business community in virtually all these cases, and has resolved these complaints informally wherever possible. Paul-André Comeau is optimistic that the CAI can continue to mediate the majority of disputes that come before it.

Real Life in the Business World

Nothing appears to be more important to privacy protection than the "organizational culture" that has developed within a company—its long-held views, practices, and values. These can cripple efforts to introduce a well-designed privacy policy if the policy is treated only as window dressing—all show and no action. Consequently, it is important for everyone, from senior management to the front line, to buy into the benefits of such a policy for the company. Awareness, education, and training are critical. One way of getting people to buy in is to show them how similar policies have benefited other companies. Pierrot Peladeau, a long-standing privacy advocate, lawyer, and business consultant, has advised many companies on how to introduce privacy policies into their organizations.

Treating information as a strategic resource is a good way to explore existing information practices and develop ways to protect privacy. When viewed in this light, discussions about privacy protection become translated into the language of information management. The management objectives that may be advanced through this approach are economy, efficiency, quality of decisions, control of information resources, and enhanced customer confidence.

Peladeau reported that a number of companies he worked with saved hundreds of thousands of dollars by introducing privacy-protective measures that overhauled their information practices. In one company, the time required to read outdated information in customers' files amounted to "a few thousand hours a year." Thousands of hours had been wasted annually collecting, compiling, and storing information that was unneeded and never used. In another example, a 19-page form was reduced to 1 page, saving considerable financial and human resources. This is why Peladeau considers data protection to be a cost-reduction tool; it saves money. He found that a manager "could easily waste up to the equivalent of a month per year in poor informational practices."[4]

In order for these savings to be achieved, responsibility for this type of review must come from a high level in the organization and must be communicated to all staff. Implementation must begin with an assessment of the business and an attempt to identify what information is essential to its operations. Then comes a thorough review of files and a revision of data collection forms. Purging all nonessential information in files is an important component of this exercise. It is followed by an assessment of any security measures in place.

The next step is for the company to turn attention to the contact points it has with its customers—people through which members, shareholders, customers, and employees can receive information, ask questions, or file a complaint. This is an important stage, because the quality of the contact you have with your customers can ultimately make or break your company. Do you tell your customers the reason you're asking for their information? Do you assure them that it won't be given to anyone else without their consent? Do you tell them that you value their information and will safeguard it, keeping it confidential and secure? Do you tell them that you have a privacy policy that gives them access to their files, and a process by which they can have errors corrected?

Peladeau said that many computer systems he has seen have been fraught with problems because they failed to take into account basic data protection considerations. Systems designers said that the problems could easily have been avoided at the outset had someone alerted them to the privacy concerns. Senior management's better understanding of the information requirements is essential to avoiding costly mistakes. And since the information highway will be "personal information-intensive," Peladeau regards data protection practices as "simply a very good investment."

An interesting finding has to do with the types of individuals within Quebec organizations who have been assigned responsibility for ensuring compliance with the law. A number of these people are heads of marketing departments, and they use the fact of protecting their customers' privacy as a marketing tool. The new message to their customers goes something like this: "We are the leaders in the field, we respect and protect your privacy. Buy from us." So there it is—the message that privacy makes for good business appears to be playing out in real life: marketing directors consider privacy a salable item and are using it in their public relations efforts.

How to Develop Your Own Privacy Policy

To help businesses develop their own privacy policies and review their information practices, we have listed some points that may be of assistance to organizations when incorporated into their day-to-day practices. These draw heavily on Fair Information Practices. (Unlike in the rest of this book, the "you" in this section is directed at the businessperson.)

External Focus: Customer Service

The 12-Step Privacy Program to Better Business Practices

1. First and foremost, *respect the privacy of your customers.* Recognize that they are the true owners of any

information they provide about themselves. Accordingly, consult them if you are developing any new policies or practices that could affect their privacy.[5]

2. *All businesses should have a policy* about their information practices, not only for good management but also to be able to communicate the policy to their customers.

3. The existence of your privacy policy should be *publicized,* and customers should be given a copy upon request. Avoid secrecy when it comes to your customers' information.

4. *Identify the primary purpose.* Always tell your customers the reason you want their personal information and what you intend to do with it. Don't collect more than you need to achieve that purpose.

5. *Get it directly.* Wherever possible, get your information directly from your customers. They are in the best position to give you the most accurate information. If you have to get some indirectly, first obtain your customers' consent. When in doubt, *think "informed consent"* (consent that is meaningful and voluntary). Let that be your guide.

6. *No secondary use without consent.* Don't use the information beyond the primary purpose—that is, for any secondary uses—without the consent of your customers. If you want to sell or rent their personal information (as in a mailing list) to a third party, don't do it without your customers' consent.

7. *How to get consent:* always provide a clear, specific opt-out clause on any form you use to gather information. This will give your customers the opportunity to tell you if they don't want you to use their information for purposes other than the primary purpose.

8. *In your opt-out clause,* make sure you tell your customers what other purposes you want to use their information for. Be specific and, if appropriate, offer them a range of selections.

9. *Don't threaten to withdraw your services* if customers don't agree to let you use their information for secondary

purposes. You'll be the loser in the long run—they'll take their business elsewhere.

10. *Think "open and accessible."* Create an atmosphere of openness by making your files open and transparent to your customers—give them easy access to their own personal information. *Never maintain any hidden files.*

11. *Correct mistakes quickly.* If something turns out to be wrong, make sure you have a process to correct the errors quickly. You will find that keeping accurate information is better for the interests of both you and your customers.

12. *Listen* to your customers' concerns.

Internal Focus: The Organizational Culture

Ten more steps, directed internally, complete the privacy program to better business practices.

13. *Tell your staff.* A company's privacy policy should be clearly communicated to all staff members, not only so that they can follow its requirements but also because their knowledge of the policy will convey a sense of confidence to customers.

14. *Create awareness.* A corporate understanding and awareness of privacy should be fostered among all employees to prevent inadvertent errors such as disclosures of information when disclosure was not known to be contrary to the policy. A point that must be driven home is that once privacy is lost, it cannot be reclaimed. The damage is done. Protections must be built in at the front end to prevent such accidental losses.

15. *Could it affect your customers' privacy?* The effect of any initiative, product, service, system, or computer program should be assessed *before it is developed.* This should become an integral part of the design stage of any new development. Once its influence on privacy is identified, the necessary protections should be built in. A *privacy-impact assessment* should become an essential component of any initiative.

16. ***Privacy shouldn't cost more.*** Adopt a policy of redress or restoration so that if any service you offer threatens to diminish the privacy of a customer, your business will provide a means to restore that privacy at no cost to the customer.

17. ***Keep it clean.*** Take reasonable steps to make sure that the information you use is accurate and up to date.

18. ***Don't keep it too long.*** Store personal information only long enough to achieve the purpose for which you collected it (or as required by law). Develop a retention schedule to guide how long you should keep various types of information.

19. ***Keep it confidential and secure.*** Adopt a reasonable standard of security, appropriate to the sensitivity of the information. For example, extremely sensitive information would require additional security measures; consider advanced techniques such as encryption and anonymization. Procedural controls may suffice for less sensitive information. Make sure a written policy is in place.

20. ***Be careful what you do with your garbage.*** How you throw out information can be important. Secure disposal practices keep information confidential right up to the last minute and may save you a lot of embarrassment. For starters, consider using shredders for paper documents containing personal information, or hire a company that will shred for you. (Innovative companies such as Eco-Shred will save you the expense of buying shredders.) Make sure you use permanent forms of disk erasure for electronic holdings of personal information.

21. ***Act responsibly; be accountable; conduct privacy audits.*** Wherever possible, designate a high-ranking individual within your organization to be responsible for overseeing your company's privacy policy. There should also be someone in the customer service department to answer questions and respond to complaints about your information practices. Hold your staff accountable for respecting your customers' privacy. Conduct periodic privacy audits to make sure your company is following its own privacy policy.

22. *Put it in the contract.* If your company enters into con-
tracts with third parties, add a carefully worded clause to
ensure that they will honor your privacy practices. Also,
clearly identify the uses of your customers' information that
are permitted. Indicate that any other uses are prohibited.

Concluding Thought

Respect your customers' privacy. Treat their information
with care. Safeguarding its confidentiality is not enough.
Develop a privacy policy that follows Fair Information
Practices. Tell your customers about your policy. It will
increase their confidence. Make sure your employees
know about the policy too. More important, make sure
they follow it. It will be worth the effort. You will gain a
noticeable edge over your competitors—and your customers will thank you for it.

Endnotes

1. Industry Canada, *Privacy and the Canadian Information
   Highway* (Ottawa: Industry Canada, October 1994), p. 16.

2. Information and Privacy Commissioner/Ontario, *Privacy
   Protection Makes Good Business Sense* (Toronto: Information
   and Privacy Commissioner/Ontario, 1994), p. 1.

3. Information Technology Association of Canada, *Privacy Issues
   and the Emerging Information Infrastructure* (Ottawa:
   Information Association of Canada, 1994), pp. 2–3.

4. Pierrot Peladeau, "Data Protection as a Cost-Reduction Tool,"
   Privacy Journal (1995).

5. Some of the points in this section have been adapted from the
   IPC's report *Privacy Protection Makes for Good Business Sense.*
   Any direct quotes used are cited.

A Call to Action

As consumers, we often feel powerless to change the status quo. But...public pressure can succeed when enough people get exercised about practices they feel to be wrong or unfair....The only way that will change is for us, as consumers and citizens, to demand...fuller disclosure, stronger privacy protections, and better security procedures.   ANN FINLAYSON AND SANDRA MARTIN
                                                      Card Tricks, 1993

A Mosaic of Solutions for Protecting Your Privacy

In our search for solutions to protecting privacy, the most important thing we have learned is that we must speak up. The second is that there is no one answer—we will need to explore a broad range of solutions and take a multifaceted approach to protecting privacy. Just as you would find a variety of tools in a toolbox, each designed to serve a different purpose, so privacy protection must be tackled with an assortment of solutions.

Among the solutions we have explored are:

- Public education and awareness that will allow you to identify when your privacy is at risk, and then to speak up
- Strong privacy laws for both the public and private sectors
- Independent privacy commissions to watch over those laws
- Voluntary privacy codes that incorporate Fair Information Practices for organizations untouched by privacy laws, or working in conjunction with such laws

- Technical standards to preserve a minimum acceptable level of privacy and data security in various sectors
- Technologies of privacy such as encryption, blind signatures, bioscrypts, protected smart cards, and network and data security
- Building privacy into all programs and systems at the design stage and making an assessment of the privacy costs a must, just as conducting an assessment of financial costs is a must.

Make Privacy a Design Goal: Privacy Impact Assessments

Some of you may scoff at the last point, at the idea of assessing the privacy costs of a new venture just as one would assess its costs in dollars. Yet if an awareness of privacy issues develops in an organization's culture, it will foster the need to assess a new program's privacy impact, comparable to a financial cost-benefit analysis. Once the effect on privacy is assessed, any protections needed can be built into the system at the beginning, and with minimal expense. If the cost to privacy is assessed to be too high, the program can easily be redesigned or rejected, with little invested into it at so early a stage.

Let's not forget what happened to Lotus Marketplace: Households. In 1990, Lotus Development Corp. was about to release a CD-ROM containing a great deal of personal information: the name, address, age, marital status, income bracket, lifestyle characteristics, and buying habits of some 120 million households. But Lotus was forced to shelve the product after 30,000 complaints were filed by consumers who objected to it as being an invasion of their privacy. They wanted to have their names and personal information removed from the disk. Lotus withdrew the product, at an estimated cost of $8 million, because it couldn't "afford a prolonged battle over consumer privacy." This example underscores the need to address privacy concerns right from the start—at the design stage. If you detect a problem up front, you can return painlessly to the drawing board, with little cost to financial or human resources, or to privacy. So make privacy a design goal, and a privacy impact assessment a must.

Such a way of thinking on the part of business may at first seem inconceivable, but instead it should be inconceivable to design a new system or consider a new venture without assessing the costs to privacy. We believe this vision is within our reach. All that is needed is the will. That's where you come in. Consumer pressure can be a force to be reckoned with.

As in the beginning of the environmental movement, a period of incubation appears to be necessary to raise people's consciousness, to develop an understanding of the issues involved and the effects they could have. We believe the same holds true for privacy. The issues need to be identified and their impact explored. We believe we are going through such a phase now. The public's awareness of the mounting threats to privacy is growing every day, as reflected in the heightened concern for privacy shown repeatedly in consumers polls and surveys. But what must follow is taking responsibility, at a personal and corporate level—responsibility for having contributed to the problem and, more important, responsibility for correcting it. For those of you who wish to preserve the privacy you enjoy today, there are steps you can take to prevent its continued erosion.

Remember that you as consumers wield the ultimate protest in a free marketplace—you can take your business elsewhere. Below is a list of some simple things you can do to protect your privacy. If each of you takes even one of these steps, it would have a dramatic effect on how government and businesses collect, store, use, and disseminate your personal information. Failing to take action may result in far greater losses down the road. The choice, as always, is yours to make.

What You Can Do: Privacy Tips

In a report on the need for privacy protection in the marketplace, *Privacy Alert: A Consumer's Guide to Privacy in the*

Marketplace, you, the consumer, are urged to "consider seriously your privacy and what it means to you when engaging in everyday transactions in the marketplace."[1] We couldn't agree more. Contemplating the following privacy tips might be a good place to start.

We have divided our tips into two levels. Level 1: The Essentials include tips you should think about incorporating into your day-to-day activities. Level 2: Important, But Less Frequent includes equally important tips that need not be practiced every day. These are followed by Telephone Tips and General Tips to round out your privacy protection program.

Level 1: The Essentials

1. *Question.* Each time people ask you for your personal information, ask them why they want it and what they will do with it. Reject rote answers such as "We've always asked for it" and "It's company policy." These are not acceptable answers; they are simply pat phrases that have little meaning. If the person doesn't know why the company needs your information or what it plans to do with it, ask to speak to someone who does.

2. Having satisfied yourself that your information is being collected for a legitimate purpose, give only the ***minimum*** amount of personal information required. For example, you may need to fill out a product warranty card to ensure that your product remains under warranty for a period of time. But you don't need to provide any additional information that may be sought for marketing purposes and is unrelated to your purchase. ***Think*** first. How are such things as your income, occupation, or date of birth related to a product warranty?

3. *Ask* who gets to see your personal information. Will anyone outside the organization have access to it?

4. *Challenge* the sale, rental, or exchange of your personal information to third parties for secondary uses beyond the immediate transaction.

5. *Look* for an opt-out box on any form seeking your personal information. If you don't want your information added to mailing lists or passed on to third parties such as direct marketers, *check it off.* If you can't find an opt-out box, *create your own.* Simply add a sentence stating that you don't want your information sold, rented, or exchanged with other organizations for purposes beyond the immediate transaction.

6. *Beware* of free coupons, special rebate offers, or contest forms. These are often popular marketing techniques used to obtain a wealth of personal information. However, you may wish to receive these special offers. In that case, give the company as little information as needed, and ask who will have access to your information.

7. Whenever possible, *pay with cash.* This will minimize the amount of information circulating about your likes, dislikes, purchases, reading habits, and so forth. New developments in the area of stored value (cash cards) and digital cash will make this easier in the years to come.

8. *Do not give* out your social security number unless it is required by law or legitimately needed. *Challenge* any denial of service when you refuse to give your number. Talk to the manager and *protest* against the practice of routinely asking for your number. Threaten to take your business elsewhere.

Level 2: Important, But Less Frequent

9. *Ask* how the company you are doing business with keeps your information confidential. What measures does it have in place to safeguard the confidentiality of your information? Does the company have a privacy policy? If yes, ask to see it. If no, ask that one be developed.

10. Periodically check up on the company's promise not to sell or rent your information to third parties (if that had been your wish). *Complain* to senior management if you learn that your information has been passed on to others contrary to your wishes, and contrary to the company's assurances that it would not do so.

11. Ask for *access* to your personal information periodically: ask to see your file to ensure that the information in it is accurate and up-to-date. If you find a mistake, bring it to the company's attention and have the company *correct* it.

12. *Visit* your credit bureau once a year to check your file. Make a mental note to do this at the same time you schedule your annual medical checkup. Your credit checkup will serve much the same purpose: it will ensure the continued health of your credit records. Make sure that any incorrect information is corrected immediately. *Return* to your credit bureau later to make certain the information has been corrected. (Look under Credit Bureau in your telephone directory for the one nearest you.)

13. *Demand* that your name, address, and telephone number be removed from mailing lists and telephone lists by calling or writing to the Direct Marketing Association at (212) 768-7277 (DMA Mail Preference Service, P.O. Box 9008, Farmingdale, NY 11735-9008) or the Canadian Direct Marketing Association at (416) 391-2362 (1 Concorde Gate, Suite 607, Don Mills, ONT M3C 3N6). *Call back* in a few months to make sure that your name has been added to the Do Not Mail/Do Not Call lists.

14. *Write* to the Medical Insurance Bureau at P.O. Box 105, Essex Station, Boston, MA 02112, USA to obtain a copy of your medical record file.

15. *Ask your doctor* who else may access your medical records outside of the office, and for what reason. Before your doctor sends your records to a third party (say, your insurance company), ask to see them. You may also want to ask if your records have ever been reviewed during an audit; indicate your wish to be notified of such a situation. Ask your doctor and other health care providers how they keep your records confidential. Ask your pharmacist too—your prescription profile may contain a great deal of sensitive, private information.

Telephone Tips

16. *Use* the Call Blocking feature whenever you want to make a call but don't want your telephone number revealed. Simply dial *67 before the number you are calling.

17. *Complain* to your local telephone company and to the FCC or CRTC any time you receive an annoying call from an automatic dialing and answering device (ADAD). These devices have been banned in Canada (and in several U.S. states) for making unsolicited calls for the purpose of solicitation.

18. *Inquire* into what uses will be made of your information when you place a call to an 800 or 900 number. These numbers may record and sell your information to telemarketers. If the service can't answer your questions or is evasive, think twice about using it. If you have any doubts, *hang up*.

19. *Remember* that your voice mail may be accessible to others; act accordingly.

General Tips

20. When using a computer network (be it a LAN or the Net), think twice before sending sensitive or confidential information by unprotected e-mail. If your message has not been encrypted, it may be intercepted. *Encrypt* or exercise caution.

21. *Spread the word.* Tell your friends and family about what steps they can take to protect their privacy. Communicate, educate, and agitate! Don't forget the value of word of mouth.

22. *Write, fax, phone, or e-mail* government representatives. Tell them that privacy issues are important to you and that you want to know what is being done to protect your privacy. Write to the heads of all organizations you do business with, especially those that don't do a good job of protecting your privacy, and complain!

23. *Join* groups such as the Electronic Privacy Information Center, Computer Professionals for Social Responsibility, Internet Privacy Coalition, Electronic Frontier Foundation, your local chapter of the Consumers Association, the Patients' Rights Association, and the Coalition for Public Access—or any group that has an interest in protecting your privacy. ***Get active, get involved.*** The choice is yours.

24. *Subscribe* to a privacy publication such as ***Privacy Journal,*** available by phone at (401) 274-7861; ***Privacy Times,*** at (202) 829-3660; or ***Privacy Files,*** at 1 (800) 922-9151.

The Choice Is Yours

Remember that choice is what it's all about—the ability to retain control over your personal information and to choose if, when, and how your information will be used. Exercise your right to choose—before you lose it altogether.

In order for the present imbalance in matters involving our privacy to be altered, a collective effort is needed. Our voices need to be heard. Such a collective effort must translate into action being taken at the administrative, procedural, and political levels, and in changes that will result in greater protections of our privacy and the security of our personal information. "If we do not enact privacy safeguards, the future is not hard to predict: the routine recording of every aspect of our personal lives. Large institutions, public and private, will come to know more about us than we know about ourselves. Who would choose to live in such a world?"[2] Before such a world is upon us, we must debate these issues and make our views known. Public debate in this area is essential. If we wish to keep parts of our private lives truly off limits from the attention of marketers, businesses, and the government, then we must convey a clear message that says, "Hands off." In the words of one expert in this area, "No area of human life is inherently too intimate, too personal, or too private for such attention."[3]

Concluding Thought

Our final word to you is one that we have repeated through-out, and that is *choice*. You should be able to preserve your ability to choose, to choose the degree of privacy you wish to have—to give it away if you don't want it, or have it pro-tected if you value it. The control of information relating to you must, with limited exceptions, ultimately rest with you. While the right to privacy is not absolute, it is a fundamen-tal human right that must be recognized and protected. Become your own privacy watchdog.

Endnotes

1. Information and Privacy Commissioner/Ontario, *Privacy Alert: A Consumer's Guide to Privacy in the Marketplace* (Toronto: Information and Privacy Commissioner/Ontario, May 1994), p. 3. We are grateful to the IPC for the checklist contained in this report, which served as a valuable resource.

2. Marc Rotenberg, "Privacy Protection," *Government Information Quarterly*, Vol. 11, No. 3, p. 254.

3. James B. Rule, "The Information Wars: The State's Struggle to Know; the Individual's Struggle to Withhold," unpublished paper, 1995, p. 9.

Selected Bibliography

Agre, Philip E. "Looking Down the Road: Transport Informatics and the New Landscape of Privacy." *Computer Professionals for Social Responsibility Newsletter,* Vol. 13, No. 3, (1995), pp. 15–20.

————. "Surveillance and Capture: Two Models of Privacy." *The Information Society,* Vol. 10 (1994), pp. 101–127.

Agre, Philip E., and Harbs, Christine A. "Social Choice About Privacy: Intelligent Vehicle-Highway Systems in the United States," *Information Technology and People,* Vol. 7, No. 4 (1994), pp. 63–90.

Alderman, Ellen, and Kennedy, Caroline. *The Right to Privacy.* New York: Alfred A. Knopf, 1995.

Alpert, Sheri. "Privacy on Intelligent Highways: Finding the Right of Way," *Santa Clara Computer and Technology Law Journal,* Vol. 11, No. 1 (March 1995), pp. 97–118.

————. "Smart Cards, Smarter Policy: Medical Records, Privacy, and Health Care Reform," *Hastings Center Report,* Vol. 23, No. 6 (1993), pp. 13–23.

Auletta, Ken. "Under the Wire: Will the Telecommunications Revolution End in Monopoly or Big Brotherhood?" *The New Yorker,* January 17, 1994.

Bacard, André. *Computer Privacy Handbook.* Berkeley, CA: Peachpit Press, 1995.

Baker, John. "Social Responsibility in the Information Age." Paper presented at the Conference on Computers, Freedom, and Privacy, San Francisco, March 1991, pp. 25–28.

Banisar, David, ed. 1994: *Cryptography and Privacy Sourcebook: Primary Documents on U.S. Encryption Policy, the Clipper*

Chip, the Digital Telephony Proposal and Export Controls. Upland, PA: Diane Publishing, 1994.

———. "Roadblocks on the Information Superhighway: Governmental Limitations on Communications Security and Privacy." *Federal Bar News and Journal,* Vol. 41, No. 7 (August 1994), pp. 495–504.

Barlow, John Perry. "A Plain Text on Crypto Policy." *Communications of the ACM,* Vol. 36, No. 11 (November 1993), pp. 21–26.

Bellotti, Victoria, and Abigail Sellen. "Design for Privacy in Ubiquitous Computing Environments," *Proceedings of the European CSCW.* Milan: Kluwer, 1993.

Bennett, Colin J. "Computers, Personal Data, and Theories of Technology: Comparative Approaches to Privacy Protection in the 1990s," *Science, Technology, and Human Values,* Vol. 16, No.1 (Winter 1991).

———. *Regulating Privacy: Data Protection and Public Policy in Europe and the United States.* New York: Cornell University Press, 1992.

———. "The Public Surveillance of Personal Data: Comparative Responses and Policy Options." Paper presented at the Symposium on Surveillance and Social Control, Queen's University, Kingston, Ontario, May 17, 1993.

———. "Implementing Privacy Codes of Practice." Report to the Canadian Standards Association, 1995.

"Big Brother on the Rise in Workplace: New Technology Damages Morale Report Argues," *Toronto Star,* August 2, 1994.

"Big Brother Wants to Take Your Picture," editorial in *Globe and Mail,* December 11, 1993.

Branscomb, Anne Wells. *Who Owns Information? From Privacy to Public Access.* New York: Basic Books, 1994.

British Columbia Freedom of Information and Privacy Association. "Bungled Bonfire of Medical Records Fuels Call for Records Protection Law," *FIPA Bulletin* (Fall 1994).

Burkert, Herbert. "Institutions of Data Protection: An Attempt at a Functional Explanation of European Data Protection Laws," *Computer Law Journal,* Vol. 3 (1981), pp. 186–188.

Burnham, David. *The Rise of the Computer State: The Threat to Our Freedoms, Our Ethics, and Our Democratic Process.* New York: Random House, 1980.

Canada/Industry Canada. *Privacy and the Canadian Information Highway: Building Canada's Information and Communications Infrastructure.* Ottawa: Industry Canada, October 1994.

Canada/Privacy Commissioner of Canada. *Drug Testing and Privacy.* Ottawa: Supply and Services, 1990.

———. *Genetic Testing and Privacy.* Ottawa: Supply and Services, 1992.

———. *Protecting Privacy on the Information Highway: Response of the Privacy Commissioner of Canada to Privacy and the Canadian Information Highway.* Ottawa: Supply and Services, December 1994.

Carroll, Jim. "Hooey: Information Highway Debunked." *Toronto Star,* September 1, 1994.

Carruthers, E. A. Presentation to the Standing Committee of the [Ontario] Legislative Assembly at Hearings on the Freedom of Information and Privacy Act, January 20, 1994.

Cavoukian, Ann. "Go Beyond Security—Build In Privacy: The Two Are Not the Same." Paper presented at the Annual CardTech/SecureTech Conference, Atlanta, Georgia, May 12–16, 1996.

Cavoukian, Ann. "Medical Privacy and the Growing World of Health-Information Networks: Can You Have Both?" Paper presented at Visions of Privacy for the Twenty-first Century: A Search for Solutions, Victoria, B.C. May 9–11, 1996.

———. "Privacy and Medicine: Poor Laws, Electronic Records, Genetic Testing." Paper presented at the National Privacy and Public Policy Symposium, Hartford, Conn., November 2–4 1995.

———. "Genetic Privacy: The Right 'Not to Know.'" Paper presented at the Tenth World Congress on Medical Law, Jerusalem, Israel, August 28–September 1, 1994.

———. "Confidentiality Issues in Genetics: The Need for Privacy." Paper presented at the Second Symposium of the Council of Europe on Bioethics, Strasbourg, France, November 30–December 2, 1993.

————. "Genetic Testing and Data Protection." Paper presented at the Thirteenth Annual Data Protection Commissioners Conference, Paris, France, October 2–4, 1991.

————. "Genetic Testing: The Ultimate Threat to Privacy." Paper presented at Access '89: An International Workshop on Access and Privacy Laws, Ottawa, April 14–16, 1989.

Chaum, David. "Achieving Electronic Privacy," *Scientific American*, August 1992, pp. 96–101.

————. "Security Without Identification: Transaction Systems to Make Big Brother Obsolete." *Journal for the Association of Computing Machinery*, Vol. 28, No. 10 (October 1985), pp. 1030–1044.

Clarke, Roger A. "Information Technology and Dataveillance," *Communications of the ACM*, Vol. 31, No. 5 (May 1988), pp. 498–512.

Clement, Andrew. "Considering Privacy in the Development of Multi-Media Communications." *Computer Supported Cooperative Work*, Vol. 2 (1994), pp. 67–88.

————. "Electronic Workplace Surveillance: Sweatshops and Fishbowls." *Canadian Journal of Information Science,* Vol. 17, No. 4 (December 1992), pp. 18–45.

Comeau, Paul-Andre. "Understanding the Quebec Privacy Legislation and Discovering How It Will Impact Your Organization." Paper presented at the Conference on Protecting Privacy in the Information Age, Toronto, October 17–18, 1994.

Commission of the European Communities, Amended Proposal for a Council Directive on the Protection of Individuals with Regard to the Processing of Personal Data and on the Free Movement of Such Data, Com (92)-SYN 287.

Council of Europe, Convention for the Protection of Individuals with Regard to Automatic Processing of Personal Data, No. 108 (January 28, 1981).

Coyne, Andrew. "The Information Highwayman Comes Riding," *Globe and Mail*, October 1, 1994.

Crawford, Rick. "Techno Prisoners," *Adbusters Quarterly* (Summer 1994), pp. 17–23.

Curry, Michael R. "Representation, a New Technology, and the Problem of Privacy: The Challenge of Geographic Information Systems." *Science, Technology, and Human Values* (under review).

"Database Marketing: Marketers Know More About You Than Ever Before...and Know How to Use It," *Business Week*, September 5, 1994.

Davies, Simon. *Big Brother: Australia's Growing Web of Surveillance.* Sydney: Simon & Schuster, 1992.

Donaldson, Molla S., and Kathleen N. Lohr, eds. "Health Data in the Information Age." Committee on Regional Health Data Networks, Institute of Medicine. Washington D.C.: National Academy Press (1994), p. 156.

Ekos Research Associates. *Privacy Revealed: The Canadian Privacy Survey.* Ottawa, Canada. Ekos Research Associates, 1993.

Electronic Privacy Information Center, *Privacy Guidelines for the National Information Infrastructure: A Review of the Proposed Principles of the Privacy Working Group,* 1994.

Ellis, David. "I Have Seen the Future, and It Works," *Toronto Star,* September 13, 1994.

Elmer-Dewitt, Philip. "Battle for the Soul of the Internet," *Time,* July 25, 1994.

Ernst and Young. *2d Annual Information Security Survey: Trends, Concerns, and Practices.* Toronto, 1994.

Fabowalä, Lola. *Voluntary Codes: A Viable Alternative to Government Legislation?* Ottawa: Public Interest Advocacy Center, May 1994.

"Federal Trade Commission's New Initiative Solidifies Its Privacy Leadership Role," *Privacy and American Business,* Vol. 2, No. 3 (October 1995).

Finlayson, Ann, and Sandra Martin. *Card Tricks: A Consumer's Survival Guide to a Cashless World.* Toronto: Penguin Books, 1994.

Flaherty, David H. "The Need for an American Privacy Protection Commission," *Government Information Quarterly,* No. 1 (1984), pp. 235–258.

————. *Protecting Privacy in Surveillance Societies: The Federal Republic of Germany, Sweden, France, Canada, and the United States*. Chapel Hill: University of North Carolina Press, 1989.

————. "On the Utility of Constitutional Rights to Privacy and Data Protection," Case Western Reserve Law Review, Vol. 41, No. 3 (1991), pp. 831–855.

————. "Privacy, Confidentiality, and the Use of Canadian Health Information for Research and Statistics." *Canadian Public Administration*, Vol. 35, No. 1 (1992), pp. 75–93.

————. "Telecommunications Privacy: A Report to the CRTC." Ottawa, May 1, 1992.

Ford, Warwick, and Brian O'Higgins. "Public Key Cryptography and Open Systems Interconnection." *IEEE Communications Magazine* (July 1992), pp. 30–36.

Fox, Linda A. "Device Locates Missing Youths," *Toronto Sun*, July 15, 1994.

Fulford, Robert. "Drilling for Data," *Marketing*, September 26, 1994.

————. "Tolerating Electronic Sweatshops," *Globe and Mail*, December 14, 1994.

Gandy, Oscar. *The Panoptic Sort: A Political Economy of Personal Information*. Boulder: Westview Press, 1993.

Garfinkel, Simson. *PGP: Pretty Good Privacy*. New York: O'Reilly and Assoc., 1995.

Gates, Bill. "Privacy: Who Should Know What About Whom," *New York Times*, September 15, 1995.

Gellman, Robert M. "Prescribing Privacy: The Uncertain Role of the Physician in the Protection of Patient Privacy," *North Carolina Law Review*, Vol. 62 (1984), pp. 255, 274–278.

————. "American Data Protection Dilemmas." *Privacy Laws and Business* (June 1993), pp. 19–22.

————. "Fragmented, Incomplete, and Discontinuous: The Failure of Federal Privacy Regulatory Proposals and Institutions," *Software Law Journal*, Vol. 6, No. 2 (1993), pp. 199–238.

————. "An American Privacy Protection Commission: An Idea

Whose Time Has Come...Again." *Government Information Quarterly*, Vol. 11, No. 3 (1994), pp. 245–247.

———. "Privacy and the National Information Infrastructure," *DM News*, August 21, 1995.

Gibb-Clark, Margot. "Tribunal Allows TD Drug Testing: Bank's Policy Called Intrusive," *Globe and Mail*, August 17, 1994.

Graham Scott, Gina. *Mind Your Own Business: The Battle for Personal Privacy*. New York: Insight Books, 1995.

Gratton Michel. "Government Continues to Duck Questions on CSE," *Toronto Sun*, October 28, 1994.

Harper, Tim. "Ottawa Stays Mum on Spies: Liberals Refuse to Lift Veil of Secrecy on Super Agency," *Toronto Star*, October 23, 1994.

Hendricks, Evan. "DMA Medical Ethics," *Privacy Times*, Vol. 14, No. 22, November 28, 1994.

———. "Gallo Introduces Privacy Bills for Marketing, SSNs," *Privacy Times*, Vol. 14, No. 12, June 20, 1994.

———. "Latest Poll Shows Public Concern over Privacy Continues to Surge," *Privacy Times*, Vol. 11, No. 21, November 19, 1991.

———. "NY Man Sues McDonald's, Boss, over Voice Mail Invasions," *Privacy Times*, Vol. 15, No. 2, January 25, 1995.

———. "QVC: Your Profile." *Privacy Times*, Vol. 14, No. 10, October 21, 1994.

———. "On-Line: Microsoft Won't Sell Customer Names, *Privacy Times*, August 2, 1995.

———. "States Challenge FCC Proposal on Caller ID," *Privacy Times*, June 30, 1995.

———. "Woman Sues Montreal Hospital over Disclosure," *Privacy Times*, June 20, 1994.

Heron, Peter. "Privacy Protection and the Increasing Vulnerability of the Public," *Government Information Quarterly*, Vol. 11, No. 3 (1994), pp. 241–244.

"The High Price of Phone Competition...and Jargon," *Toronto Star*, September 23, 1994.

Hoeffel, Janet C. "The Dark Side of DNA Profiling: Unreliable Scientific Evidence Meets the Criminal

Defendant," *Stanford Law Review,* Vol. 42, No. 465 (1990), pp. 533–534.

Hunter, Lawrence, and James B. Rule. "Toward Property Rights in Personal Information." Paper presented to the Information and Privacy Commission/Ontario, December 17, 1993.

Information Technology Association of Canada. *Privacy Issues and the Emerging Information Infrastructure.* Ottawa: Information Technology Association of Canada, 1994.

"Is Anything Safe in Cyberspace?" *U.S. News & World Report,* January 23, 1995.

International Labor Office. "Workers' Privacy," *Conditions of Work Digest.* Geneva, 1993.

Kelly, Kevin. "Cypherpunks, E-Money," *Whole Earth Review* (Summer 1993), pp. 40–59.

Kolata, Gina. "When Patients' Records Are Commodities for Sale," *New York Times,* November 15, 1995.

Krever, Justice Horace. *Report of the Commission of Inquiry into the Confidentiality of Health Information.* Toronto: J.C. Thatcher, 1980.

Larson, Erik. *The Naked Consumer: How Our Private Lives Become Public Commodities.* New York: Henry Holt, 1992.

Laudon, Kenneth C. *The Dossier Society: Value Choices in the Design of National Information Systems.* New York: Columbia University Press, 1986.

———. "Markets and Privacy." Paper presented at the Annual Conference on Privacy and Business, Washington, D.C., October 5, 1994.

Lawson, Ian. *Privacy and Free Enterprise.* Ottawa: Public Interest Advocacy Center, December 1992.

Levy, Steven. *Hackers: Heroes of the Computer Revolution.* New York: Delta, 1994.

———. "Prophet of Privacy," *Wired Magazine* (November 1994), p. 128.

Linowes, David F. *Privacy in America: Is Your Private Life in the Public Eye?* Champaign: University of Illinois Press, 1989.

Louis Harris and Associates. *The Equifax Canada Report on Consumers and Privacy in the Information Age.* Toronto: Louis Harris and Associates, 1992.

Love, James P. Submission to the Senate Committee on Labor and Human Resources, S. 1360 Hearings held by Nancy Kassenbaum, November 14, 1995.

Lyon, David. *The Electronic Eye: The Rise of Surveillance Society.* Minneapolis: University of Minnesota Press, 1994.

Madsen, Wayne. *Handbook of Personal Data Protection.* New York: Stockton Press, 1992.

Markoff, John. "Hacker Underscores Internet's Vulnerability," *New York Times,* February 17, 1995.

Marx, Gary T. "Communications Advances Raise Privacy Concerns," *Christian Science Monitor,* January 2, 1992.

———. "New Telecommunications Technologies Require New Manners." *Telecommunications Policy.* Vol. 18, No. 7 (1994), pp. 538–551.

———. *Undercover: Police Surveillance in America.* Berkeley: University of California Press, 1988.

Mayers, Adam. "Alias Is Moving Fast on the Information Highway," *Toronto Star,* September 3, 1994.

"More Firms Buy Computer Shopping," *Toronto Star,* September 8, 1994.

Needham, Alan R. "The SIN Was Born in Shame," *Ottawa Citizen,* May 2, 1994.

Negroponte, Nicholas. *Being Digital.* New York: Knopf, 1995.

———. "Less Is More: Interface Agents as Digital Butlers," *Wired Magazine,* (June 1994), p. 142.

———. "Prime Time Is My Time," *Wired Magazine* (August 1994), p. 134.

Neumann, Peter G. "Computer Insecurity." *Issues in Science and Technology* (Fall 1994), pp. 50–54.

———. *Computer Related Risks.* New York: ACM Press, 1995.

"No Hiding Place: The Technologies That Make Life Easier Are Eroding People's Privacy," *The Economist,* August 7, 1993, pp. 16–17.

Noam, Eli. "Privacy in Telecommunications: Markets, Rights, and Regulations," in *Ethics in Telecommunications.* Cleveland: Office of the United Church of Christ, 1994.

Nussbaum, Karen. "Workers Under Surveillance." *Computerworld,* Vol. 36, No. 1 (January 6, 1992), p. 21.

OECD. *Guidelines Governing the Protection of Privacy and Transborder Flows of Personal Data.* Paris: OECD, 1981.

Ontario/Information and Privacy Commissioner. *Electronic Identification in the Information Age.* Toronto: Office of the Information and Privacy Commissioner/Ontario, 1994.

———. *Privacy Alert: A Consumer's Guide to Privacy in the Marketplace.* Toronto: Office of the Information and Privacy Commissioner/Ontario, May 1994.

———. *Privacy and Computer Matching.* Toronto: Office of the Information and Privacy Commissioner/Ontario, January 1991.

———. *Privacy Protection Principles for Electronic Mail Systems.* Toronto: Information and Privacy Commissioner/Ontario, February 1994.

Packard, Vance. *The Naked Society.* New York: Pocket Books, 1964.

Patients' Rights Association. *Access to Records Project,* 1994.

Pearlman, Mitchell. "Who Will Control the Information Highway?" *Hartford Courant,* October 20, 1993.

Peladeau, Pierrot. "Data Protection Saves Money." *Privacy Journal,* Vol. 21, No. 8 (June 1995).

———. "Implementation of a Program for Protection of Personal Information." Paper presented at the Conference on Protecting Privacy in the Information Age, Toronto, October 17–18, 1994.

Petrocelli, William. *Low Profile: How to Avoid the Privacy Invaders.* New York: McGraw-Hill, 1982.

Pollock, James. "Database Marketing: Marketing One-to-One," *Marketing,* September 26, 1994.

"Privacy: Junk-Mail Hater Seeks Profits from Sale of His Name," *Wall Street Journal,* October 13, 1995.

Raab, Charles D., and Colin J. Bennett. "Protecting Privacy Across Borders: European Policies and Prospects," *Public Administration,* Vol. 72, No. 1 (Spring 1994).

RAM Mobile Data. "The Inherent Security of Data over Mobitex Wireless Packet Data Networks," *RAM Mobile Data White Paper,* August 1994.

Regan, Priscilla M. *Legislating Privacy: Technology, Social Values, and Public Policy*, Chapel Hill: University of North Carolina Press, 1995.

Regan, Priscilla M. "The Globalization of Privacy: Implications of Recent Changes in Europe," *American Journal of Economics and Society*, No. 257 (1993), pp. 264–265.

Reidenberg, Joel R. "Privacy in the Information Economy: A Fortress or Frontier for Individual Rights?" *Federal Communications Law Journal*, Vol. 44, No. 2 (1993), pp. 195–243.

———. "U.S. Business Practice in the Absence of a General Data Protection Law." Paper presented at Privacy Laws and Business Seventh Annual Conference, Cambridge, England, July 11, 1994.

Rheingold, Howard. *The Virtual Community: Homesteading on the Electronic Frontier*. Reading, Mass.: Addison Wesley, 1993.

Rifkin, Jeremy. "Efforts to Improve the Human Race." TVOntario transcripts of *Biotechnology: Blessing or Curse?* (1988).

Riley, Thomas B. "Information Technology and Privacy Protection." Paper presented at the Conference on Privacy and Technology, Ottawa, September 30, 1994.

Rosenberg, Jerry M. *The Death of Privacy*. New York: Random House, 1969.

Rotenberg, Marc. "Communications Privacy: Implications for Network Design," *Communications of the ACM*, Vol. 36, No. 8 (August 1993), pp. 61–68.

———. "Information Policy: Electronic Privacy Legislation in the United States," *Journal of Academic Librarianship* (September 1994), pp. 227–230.

———. "Privacy Protection," *Government Information Quarterly*, Vol. 11, No. 3 (1994), pp. 253–254.

———. "Wiretapping Bill: Costly and Intrusive." *Insight*, October 24, 1994.

———. "Inside the Beltway: The Politics of Privacy." *Government Information Insider* (Fall 1995).

Rothfedder, Jeffrey. *Privacy for Sale: How Computerization Has Made Everyone's Private Life an Open Secret.* New York: Simon & Schuster, 1992.

Rowan, Geoffrey. "Snoopophobia Haunts Information Highway: 85% Fear New Network Will Mean Loss of Privacy," *Globe and Mail*, May 3, 1994.

Rule, James B. *Private Lives and Public Surveillance: Social Control in the Computer Age.* New York: Schocken Books, 1974.

———. "The Information Wars: The State's Struggle to Know; The Individual's Struggle to Withhold." Unpublished paper, 1995.

Rule, James B., Douglas McAdam, Linda Stearns, and David Uglow. *The Politics of Privacy: Planning for Personal Data Systems as Powerful Technologies.* New York: Elsevier, 1980.

Samarajiva, Rohan. "The Democratic Test Is: Can Individuals Negotiate Their Own Boundary Conditions in Telecoms?" *Intermedia*, Vol. 22, No. 1 (February 1994), pp. 34–43.

———. "Privacy in Electronic Public Space: Emerging Issues," *Canadian Journal of Communications*, Vol. 19 (1994), pp. 87–99.

Schneier, Bruce. *Applied Cryptography: Protocols, Algorithms, and Source Code in C.* New York: John Wiley & Sons, 1994.

Schoeman, Ferdinand D., ed. *Philosophical Dimensions of Privacy: An Anthology.* Cambridge: Cambridge University Press, 1984.

Schwartau, Winn. *Information Warfare: Chaos on the Electronic Superhighway.* New York: Thunder's Mouth Press, 1995.

Schwartz, Paul M. "Data Processing and Government Administration," *Hastings Law Journal*, Vol. 43, No. 1321 (1992).

———. Testimony of Paul Schwartz to the Government Information, Justice, and Agriculture Subcommittee of the House Committee on Government Operations, House of Representatives, 103rd Congress, May 4, 1994.

———. "The Protection of Privacy in Health Care Reform," *Vanderbilt Law Review*, Vol. 48, No. 2 (March 1995).

Seipp, David J. *The Right to Privacy in American History.* Cambridge, Mass.: Harvard University Press, 1978.

Shaw, Erin, John Westwood, and Russell Wodell. *The Privacy Handbook: A Practical Guide to Your Privacy Rights in British Columbia and How to Protect Them.* Vancouver: Canadian Reprography Collective, 1994.

Simitis, Spiros. "Reviewing Privacy in an Information Society." *University of Pennsylvania Law Review,* Vol. 135 (1987), pp. 707–746.

Smith, H. Jeff. *Managing Privacy: Information Technology and Corporate America.* Chapel Hill: University of North Carolina Press, 1994.

Smith, Robert Ellis. "Some Are More Equal than Others," *Privacy Journal,* Vol. 22, No. 1 (November 1995).

———. "Implanting ID Microchips in Humans No Longer Far-Fetched." *Privacy Journal,* Vol. 20, No. 8 (June 1994).

———. "Modest Awards for Average Citizens Whose Privacy Was Invaded." *Privacy Journal,* Vol. 20, No. 12 (October 1994).

———. *Our Vanishing Privacy (and What You Can Do to Protect Yourself).* Port Townsend: Loompanics Unlimited, 1993.

———. "Paid to Watch Ads?" *Privacy Journal,* Vol. 20, No. 10 (August 1994).

Smith, Robert Ellis, with Eric Siegel and James S. Sulanowski. *War Stories: Accounts of Persons Victimized by Invasions of Privacy.* rev. 2d ed. Providence: 1993.

Stallings, William. *Protect Your Privacy: A Guide for PGP Users.* Englewood Cliffs, N.J.: Prentice-Hall, 1995.

Stern, Leonard. "Information Highway Ride Lands Parolee in Ottawa Jail," *Ottawa Citizen,* February 18, 1995.

Stoll, Clifford. *Silicon Snake Oil: Second Thoughts on the Information Highway.* New York: Doubleday, 1995.

Sussman, Vic. "Policing Cyberspace: Cops Want More Power to Fight Cybercriminals," *U.S. News & World Report,* January 23, 1995.

Suzuki, David, and P. Knutson. *Genethics: The Ethics of Engineering Life.* Don Mills, Ont.: Stoddart Publishing, 1988.

Swainson, Gail. "Report Slams Metro Police for Dossiers on Black Activists," *Toronto Star,* June 24, 1994.

Tapscott, Don, and Art Caston. *Paradigm Shift: The New Promise of Information Technology.* New York: McGraw-Hill, 1993.

———. "How to Avoid Information Apartheid," in *On Ramp: Your Guide to the Information Highway.* Toronto: Globe and Mail, 1994.

———. *The Digital Economy: Promise and Peril in the Age of Networked Intelligence.* New York: McGraw-Hill, 1995.

Tomko, George J. *Mytec Technologies Annual Report,* Toronto, Ontario, 1994.

Toulin, Alan. "Tribunal OKs Drug Tests for Jobs," *Financial Post,* August 17, 1994.

Tremayne-Lloyd, Tracey. "Access and Privacy of Health Care Information." Paper presented at McMaster University Hospital, Hamilton, Ontario, June 17, 1994.

U.S. Congress, Office of Technology Assessment (OTA). *Federal Government Information Technology: Electronic Record Systems and Individual Privacy.* Washington D.C.: GPO, 1986.

———. *Protecting Privacy in Computerized Medical Information.* Washington, D.C.: GPO, 1993.

U.S. General Accounting Office. "Computer Matching: Quality of Decisions and Supporting Analyses Little Affected by 1988 Act." Report to the Chairman, Information, Justice, Transportation, and Agriculture Subcommittee, Committee on Government Operations, House of Representatives, October 1993, GAO/PEMD-94-2.

U.S. Privacy Protection Study Commission. *Personal Privacy in an Information Society.* Washington, D.C.: GPO, 1977.

U.S. Department of Health, Education, and Welfare. "Records, Computers, and the Rights of Citizens." Report of the Secretary's Advisory Committee on Automated Personal Data Systems. Washington, D.C.: Department of Health, Education, and Welfare, 1973.

Velazquez, Nydia M. "Privacy, Confidentiality, and Security Provisions of HR 3600." Testimony to the U.S. Senate Judiciary Committee, January 27, 1994.

Warren, Samuel, and Louis Brandeis. "The Right to Privacy," *Harvard Law Review*, Vol. 4 (1890), pp. 193–220.

Westin, Alan F. *Privacy and Freedom*. New York: Atheneum, 1967.

Westin, Alan F., and Michael A. Baker. *Databanks in a Free Society: Computers, Record-Keeping, and Privacy*. New York: Quadrangle Books, 1972.

"Who's Reading Your Medical Records?" *Consumer Reports* (October 1994), pp. 628–632.

Wickens, Barbara. "New Technology Has Made Trafficking in Personal Data a Huge Industry," *Maclean's*, April 26, 1993, pp. 20–22.

Index

ABOUT THE AUTHORS

ANN CAVOUKIAN, PH.D., is Assistant Commissioner of the
Information and Privacy Commission of Ontario, Canada. An
expert in the field of privacy and data protection, she has written
and lectured extensively about this subject around the world.

DON TAPSCOTT is an international consultant, speaker, and writer
on the topic of information technology. He is the Chairman of the
Alliance for Converging Technologies, a think tank conducting a
multimillion dollar investigation into the digital media and their
impact on business and society. Tapscott is the author of five
books, including the best-selling *Paradigm Shift* and *The Digital
Economy: Promise and Peril in the Age of Networked Intelligence*,
both published by McGraw-Hill. He is based in Toronto, Canada.